I WANT MY PEOPLE WELL

by

pablo flotho

CONTENTS

DEDICATION

To, Mary the wife of my youth, who has stuck with me through the best of times and the worst of times.

Introduction

A few months before I became a believer, I returned home from work in the afternoon. My wife, Mary, who was already a believer, was listening to a tape of some preacher. Something about it caught my attention and later, when she left to go to the market, I began to listen to the tape. The preacher, whom I found out later, was Fred Price, the pastor of a large congregation in Southern California, was preaching on healing. I didn't need healing, but something about his boldness and confidence with which he spoke, captured my attention. As I listened to the tape, I realized that he was absolutely convinced of the truth of that which he was speaking. At that time I barely believed in God. Although I didn't doubt the historical existence of Jesus, I certainly didn't believe that Jesus was the son of God, and I thought most preachers were probably charlatans or perhaps somewhat deluded.

Later on, after I became a believer, I attended this man's church. At the end of the service a young boy, about eight years old, came forward accompanied by his grandmother and the young boy testified that after someone had laid hands on him in that church the previous Sunday, his eye, which had been blind, was now seeing. The boy's grandmother corroborated his story and the boy covered his good eye with his hand and read from a fine print Bible to demonstrate his healing. The crowd went ballistic! I became interested in healing and miracles even before I was a believer because I felt that if an individual could pray for someone and a miracle happened in his life, surely the person that he prayed to must have been listening and possessed not only the power to get the job done but the compassion to motivate him to do so. I concluded that, if the God of heaven, the creator of the universe would bother hearing the prayers of mere mortals like us, that meant He was concerned for us and cared about our future.

Later on that summer, I attended a conference in another church in southern California, and heard the same man teach for five days straight on the subject of divine healing. Again, I was struck by the boldness and confidence that this man had in God's word. It was said of Jesus, "He spoke with authority, and not as the scribes." My heart was captured by this teaching on the supernatural power of God. I sensed a still small voice on the inside saying, "You can do that." Now I know that voice was the Holy Spirit speaking on the inside of me but then I wasn't sure what it was and I ignored the voice, thinking, that surely couldn't be God speaking to me, because I was convinced that only some special anointed servants of God could pray for the sick and get results.

Soon after that, the Holy Spirit spoke to Mary and me, indicating that we should move to Southern California and attend Bible College in the city of Anaheim. That church held a miracle service every Thursday morning, which was attended by about two thousand people. I was there almost every Thursday and saw hundreds of miracles take place. Soon I was invited to be part of the group that worked in the prayer room of the church. I was often called upon to pray for the sick, who would appear in the five hundred seat prayer room after the service on Thursday and Sunday morning. We were given ten minutes to minister to the sick; five minutes for an explanation of Biblical healing and five minutes to pray for all the people. Often there would be fifty or more people that would come for healing. The time constraints made it really impossible to stop and ask each person what they needed and to pray a personal prayer for each individual. We simply laid hands on the sick people and perhaps, ask one or two what was their particular problem. The Holy Spirit instructed me that I was not to ask anyone if they felt better after they were prayed for. I was simply to lay hands on them according to, Mark 16:18; which says, *"that believers will lay hands on the sick and they shall recover"*, and I was to believe therefore that they were healed as soon as I prayed for them.

I ministered to sick people once and sometimes, twice a week for approximately three months. During that period of time, no one came back to report having been healed. Because of that, I became extremely discouraged, I complained to the Lord saying, "You picked the wrong guy, I must not be called to pray for the sick because in all this time no one has gotten healed." The Holy Spirit asked me, "What did I instruct you to do?" I answered, "You said, I was to lay hands on the sick and to believe that they were healed as soon as I did that." Then he said, "What is your problem then, aren't you doing what I told you to do?" "Yes," I said, "but in all this time I don't know if anyone was healed." Again the Holy Spirit replied, "Your job is to lay your hands on the sick and to believe that they are healed, my job is to do the healing." I continued on for several months after that, praying for the sick every time I had an opportunity. I think that went on for about nine months and I prayed for several hundred people before someone actually came to me, and told me that they had received healing, when I prayed for them. I also noticed that, when other people on the prayer teams would pray for the sick, that people would often fall under the power of God. Whereas, when I would pray, hardly anyone would fall down and I was seldom conscious of any anointing or any particular sense of God's presence. This was disturbing but I realized later that Jesus was teaching me to pray for the sick by faith, in His word, and not by feelings.

Finally, after about a year, a few started to come back and report that they had been healed. This took place in an ever increasing manner. Since then, we have prayed for many thousands of people in a dozen different countries. We've seen hundreds healed in a single service but more importantly, we release others to pray for the sick as well.

I was first challenged by John Wimber, the founder of the Vineyard movement, to train and release others to minister to the sick and oppressed. I remember well attending a service at Canyon High School in 1978 and seeing John run a healing service. After teaching for a while, John announced, "Now we're going to do some healing. Is there anyone out there who God has impressed with a word of knowledge?" A girl stood up and gave a detailed word about a healing that was taking place. Then he asked the audience, who had the particular infirmity that was revealed by the word of knowledge. He asked those persons to stand up and invited those around them to lay hands on them and pray for healing. Within a few minutes there were about a dozen such circles of prayer around the auditorium. Later he invited people to come to the front and give testimony to the things that they had been healed of. There were several healings that took place. I remember thinking, I have been teaching for years that all God's children can heal the sick, but this guy is doing it." The Holy Spirit used this occurrence to

8

encourage me to begin to train others how to pray for the sick and not just do it myself while they watched.

As you are reading this book, it is almost a certainty that parts of it will upset you and maybe, at first you will not embrace the teaching. That is normal, especially for those who have been trained in systems that either ignore or oppose all present day activity of the Holy Spirit in the church. Don't throw the book out, but go back to the parts of the book that bothered you the most and wrestle with the material. Pray and ask Jesus to give you revelation of his truth. Pray Paul's prayer found in Ephesians 1:15-17 for yourself daily. Look up scripture and try to honestly consider the entire picture. Avoid the temptation to "proof text" the word. Proof-texting is finding one verse or part of a verse that seems to be saying what you have always believed and cling to that text, ignoring other material and ignoring the entire thread of teaching through the New Testament. If after diligent study, you are convinced that I am in error, write me an email at the address found at the end of the book and present your case in the peace, love and joy of the Lord and we can reason together. As all Bible teachers, I am an imperfect vessel but open to being corrected by scripture, but not by human opinion.

Also, ask yourself this question. "Is the way I have always believed and interpreted the Bible producing results in my life?" If the answer is "no", then perhaps a change of methods would be in order for you. The writer of Hebrews said that we should be followers of those who through faith and patience inherit the promises. (6:12) There are multitudes of pastors, priests, Bible teachers, prophets and apostles that want us to follow what they

believe about the Bible, but ask yourself, "Are they inheriting the promises?"
If not, then don't follow them.

Late one night I returned to my room after a long meeting in a Central American country. I had prayed for a large number of sick people and was exhausted. Before I laid down, I got down on my knees and thanked the Lord for all the people who had been healed and saved that night. The response I got from the Lord was unusual and I have never forgotten it. He said, **"I want my people well."** It was a simple statement that could easily be passed by without much thought, but it was so clear and I could detect the emotion that it contained. I don't know how to describe to you what that word did to me, but it was a life changing experience that has stuck in my spirit. Just as an earthly father wants his own children well and experiences anguish and pain to see them suffer, I could sense the anguish and pain in the voice of the Lord with this word. Never again did I entertain any doubt as to the will of God for healing. He wants his people well!

CHAPTER ONE

DOES GOD STILL HEAL TODAY?

Many years ago, I was teaching the Bible at a house meeting in Mexico City. My subject was divine healing. At that time, I had only been teaching on healing for a few years. I noticed a woman who seemed very intense. She was frantically taking notes about everything I said. I thought that maybe she was very excited about the teaching but I found out later that the reason she was taking notes was so that she could prove that I was teaching false doctrine. It turned out that she was the wife of a pastor who's denomination did not believe that God was working miracles, healing or delivering people in the present day. She told me, later, that she had gone through my teaching in great detail trying to find fault with something I had taught and that, even though she was trained in theology, she was unable to find anything unscriptural in the teaching. It was obvious that she had approached the scripture with an open mind and the Holy Spirit was able to reveal the truth to her. Lamentably, there are many whose hearts are not open to the Holy Spirit and they cling tenaciously to the false teachings that they have received in the past. I pray that your heart is open and that you're willing to listen to the voice of the Holy Spirit. The word of God promises that He will reveal truth from God's Word, to the hungry.

THE BIBLE AS THE WORD OF GOD

Before we begin the study of divine healing, it is imperative that we settle one issue, that of the integrity of God's written word. We can hear teaching on any subject day and night but it will not profit us unless we first believe that the Bible is a divinely inspired document, written for the purpose of revealing Christ to us and God's will for our lives. Many Christians today have an extremely weak concept of the Bible as God's word. The only sure revelation of what God says and who He is, is what we find written in the pages of the Bible.

"For the word of God is living and powerful, and sharper than any two-edged sword, piercing even to the division of soul and spirit, and of joints and marrow, and is a discerner of the thoughts and intents of the heart." (Hebrews 4:12)

The power, integrity and trustworthiness of God's word can be seen from Genesis to Revelation. The Bible is a compendium of sixty-six different books by numerous different authors, written over a period of probably two thousand years and all telling the same story, the story of God the Father and His son, Jesus Christ. It relates the stories of many different people who knew God, decided to trust God, and obey what He instructed them to do and they each testify to the end result that their lives were changed for the better. They were blessed and in the end they were glad that they had done it.

We see the results of God's speaking in Genesis. We see that the earth was created out of nothing except the power of the Holy Spirit acting on God's command and creation happened.
"In the beginning God created the heavens and the earth. The earth was without form, and void; and darkness was on the face of the deep. And the Spirit of God was hovering over the face of the waters. Then God said, "Let there be light"; and there was light." (Gen. 1:1-3)

The important thing is that God spoke and things happened. God has not stopped speaking and things have not quit responding to the effect of his word.

Many believers put more confidence in a prophetic word given by a brother or sister in a gospel meeting than in the clearly stated promises of the Bible. I cannot prove conclusively to you, in this brief writing that the Bible is true and worthy of trust, I can only challenge you to take the "60 day free trial offer." Seriously, there are many who battled doubt and unbelief for years and years without ever resolving the issue that we're speaking of. The only way you'll ever be able to resolve this issue is to step out in faith and trust the Lord, put Him to the test, and see if He doesn't come through for you. The Bible says *"taste and see that the Lord is good."* So, try it for 60 days. Study the New Testament, Matthew Mark Luke and John, the record of Jesus' doings on earth. Study his promises, study his acts, study his attitudes, how He responded to people, how He responded to unbelieving Pharisees (the religious leaders of the day). Begin to pray and ask Jesus for what you need based on the promises of the Bible. I believe Jesus will respond to you and you won't have to ask for your return on the "money back guarantee."

There are some however, who have been trained in unbelief, and negative systems, and they will have to unlearn a lot of the things that they learned in Sunday school or church services about healing, " why it isn't for today, and why it won't work for you", before you will be able to begin learning what the Bible really teaches. If you have been trained in cessationist[1] and dispensationalist theology (see Appendix I), you will have to read the Bible as if you've never read it before. Ask Jesus to give you revelation of His truth. There are many who have been taught that after the apostolic period, God removed His healing and miracle working power from the Church. The pastors and teachers who assert that, today God is doing no works of a supernatural character, are in grave error. Neither the Bible nor history supports such a belief.

THE TESTIMONY OF CHURCH HISTORY
The belief that God has removed his supernatural power from the Church is not only unscriptural but it is not supported by history.

The history of the Church is filled with reports of miracles, healings, prophesies, and many supernatural occurrences, from the earliest church fathers to the present day. Early church fathers such as Justin Martyr, Clement of Rome, Polycarp, Tertullian, Antony, and other Church leaders during the first four centuries, spoke openly and clearly about healings, miracles, and even gave specific instructions for expelling demonic spirits. Agustin is the first who makes a case for the cessation of supernatural gifts in the fourth century. In Agustin's later writings he recanted his position and admitted that God, indeed, worked miracles in the present day. Later, in the time of the reformation, we find witnesses like George Fox, George Wishart, John Knox, (16c), John Welch, (17c) Jeanne Guyon, Jonathan Edwards, George Whitfield (18c) C.H. Spurgeon, Charles Finney and Padre Pio (an Italian

---

[1] Those who believe that miracles passed away after the death of the last of the twelve apostles

14

Catholic monk who performed thousands of healings) (19c) D.L. Moody, and others, too numerous to count in the twentieth century, who all saw the miracle working power of God in operation. Some of the above did not come to the place of viewing the supernatural activity of God as normal, but at least they saw and reported supernatural activity in their day. Others like Edward Irving (19c) Charles Parham, Stephen Jeffreys, Maria Woodworth-Etter, (19-20 C) not only allowed but encouraged the supernatural activity of the Holy Spirit in their meetings.

A thorough study of Church history reveals that there is no century during the history of the Church when there was no demonstration of the supernatural confirming God's Word with signs and wonders.
I include one quote as an example from the Journal of George Fox (1694-1691) the founder of the Friends Church.

"After some time I went to a meeting at Arnside, where was Richard Myer, who had been long lame of one of his arms. I was moved of the Lord to say unto him amongst all the people, 'Stand up upon thy legs,' for he was sitting down. And he stood up, and stretched out his arm that had been lame a long time, and said, 'Be it known unto you, all people, that this day I am healed.' Yet his parents could hardly believe it; but after the meeting was done, they had him aside, took off his doublet, (brace) and then saw it was true." [2]

---

[2] George Fox, an autobiography: Ed. Rufus M. Jones, M.A., Litt. D. p.103,4

This incident was not a rare occurrence. Fox's journal is full of the supernatural; healings, deliverance, words of knowledge, discerning of spirits, and miracles of divine protection and judgment on opposers of the gospel.

Every century of the last two thousand years of Church history contains accounts of supernatural phenomena, healing, deliverance from demonic powers, miracles of diverse kinds. Yet there have always been some who wished to silence the testimony of God claiming that miracles had passed away, some even claiming that they never really happened.

The cessationists are not, however, the worst enemies of the truth. The worst enemies of the truth are those who have a small place in their doctrinal scheme for the present day operation of the Holy Spirit in healings and miracles, but these are not a part of their ongoing practice. These movements and denominations add fuel to the fire of those who would oppose all present day miracles. If we truly believe in something, then we must practice it. We must pay whatever price necessary to obtain the promise of God's manifested presence in our midst in the present day. Few churches today cultivate the manifested presence of the Holy Spirit in their midst, and many who do, have become more interested in extra biblical phenomena like the appearance of gemstones, gold dust, oil oozing out of someone's Bible, the testimonies of people who have supposedly taken trips to the third heaven or some other strange occurrences, instead of concentrating on the simple gospel and what is biblically supernatural.

Conclusion

So we see that there is neither validity to the argument, nor any scriptural basis for the belief that healing and miracles have been done away with. We have also seen that Church history is filled with compelling testimony of healing and miracles in every generation. Any Bible believing Christian who has been trained in cessationist and dispensationalist beliefs should seriously reconsider his beliefs in the light of clear scriptural teaching and historical fact.

CHAPTER TWO

IS HEALING FOR ALL?

MAT 8:16,17; *When evening had come, they brought to Him many who were demon- possessed. And He cast out the spirits with a word, and healed all who were sick, 17 that it might be fulfilled which was spoken by Isaiah the prophet, saying: "He Himself took our infirmities and bore our sicknesses."*

When I was a seminary student, one of my professors told a story of a close friend of his who had a harsh character and temperament. The professor said that his wife suffered a long and difficult battle with cancer and later died and that his friend, through this experience, became a much softer and compassionate person. The professor's conclusion was that it was the will of God that this poor fellow's wife die of cancer in order to teach him humility and compassion. When I heard this, I was somewhat shaken in my confidence in the healing power of God. I was a very young believer and I had been studying the subject of divine healing diligently, but was still in doubt about some concepts. At the same time, my wife and I, along with three children were living in an 18-foot trailer (6 m. long) and at that time, all my children were sick with the flu. I took my Bible and a jug of water and went out to a secluded mountain area, not too far from where we were living. I sat down on a big rock near a creek there and told the Lord, "I have to have your word on this thing of healing. Is it or is it not your will to heal all your children! And if it's really your plan to train your children through sickness, like my professor says, then I need to

19

know that also." Then I began to pray in other tongues. I had learned that when we speak in other tongues that we communicate directly with God, spirit to Spirit. (1Cor. 14) I spent several hours praying in other tongues and after about six hours the Lord spoke to me and said, "Get your Bible and open it..." He took me through about an hour of Bible study and showed me four different biblical ways that God teaches and trains his children. That day and the next changed my whole life. Since then no one has been able to shake my belief in healing as the birthright of God's children. The clear revelation of the will of God regarding healing is as real to me as my own existence. It is imperative that we go to God directly and receive from Him through His written word and by the Spirit, the clear revelation of truth. Later I will deal with some of the details of what He taught me on that day.

The first question we need to find an answer to if we desire to be healed and to take healing to others, is this one: **Is healing for all?** Is it really God's desire to extend healing power to all His children? In the above passage it says that Jesus "...healed all that were sick..." We must find the answer to this question, because if we maintain doubt in our hearts as to the will of God in this matter, we will not have the faith necessary to receive healing from Him. It is faith in God's promises that secures the answer to our prayers. Most Christians believe that God can heal, many believe that He may occasionally decide to heal someone but few really believe that healing should be a normal, everyday occurrence in the lives of believers worldwide. Without faith, James tells us, we should not expect to receive anything from God. (James1:6)

Faith begins when we know the will of God. The only reliable source for knowing the will of God is The Holy Bible. The Bible is the will of God.

The apostle John tells us, " *Now this is the confidence that we have in Him, that if we ask anything according to His will, He hears us. And if we know that He hears us, whatever we ask, we know that we have the petitions that we have asked of Him.*" (1John 5:14,15)

Therefore if we ask, petition, pray according to the promises found in the Bible we can be assured that we will receive the answer.

There are many who believe that God heals. Many believe that, occasionally, someone might be healed by God. They just don't believe that God desires to heal all His children, and as we will see later, to keep them well all the time.

If you make a diligent study of the Gospels (Mathew, Mark, Luke and John) and decide to believe everything that is taught in those books about and by Jesus, you can't help but come to the conclusion that He sees sickness as an enemy of God and of His kingdom, and that it is His will to heal every sick person. In the gospel of Matthew there are eight different occasions where Jesus healed everyone who came to him in certain places. Let's look at some of those texts. Please don't become impatient and skip ahead. Read each one of these eight texts carefully and study them, especially if you need healing because, "*...faith come by hearing and hearing by the word of God.*" (Ro.10:17) In fact it would be better if you would look them up in your own Bible and study them in their context, and underline the passages so that you might

21

easily find them again.

MAT 4:24 *Then His fame went throughout all Syria; and they brought to Him all sick people who were afflicted with various diseases and torments, and those who were demon-possessed, epileptics, and paralytics; and **He healed them**.*

8:16 *When evening had come, they brought to Him many who were demon- possessed. And He cast out the spirits with a word, **and healed all who were sick**, 17 that it might be fulfilled which was spoken by Isaiah the prophet, saying: "He Himself took our infirmities and bore our sicknesses."*

9:35 *And Jesus went about all the cities and villages, teaching in their synagogues, preaching the gospel of the kingdom, **and healing every sickness and every disease among the people**. 36 But when He saw the multitudes, He was moved with compassion for them, because they were weary and scattered, like sheep having no shepherd.*

12:15 *"But when Jesus knew it, He withdrew from there; and great multitudes followed Him, and **He healed them all**."*

14:14 *"And when Jesus went out He saw a great multitude; and He was moved with compassion for them, **and healed their sick**."*

14:35,36; *"And when the men of that place recognized Him, they sent out into all that surrounding region, brought to Him all who were sick, 36 and begged Him that they might only touch the hem of His garment. And **as many as touched it were made perfectly well**."*

15:30,31; *"Then great multitudes came to Him, having with them those who were lame, blind, mute, maimed, and many others; and they laid them down at Jesus' feet, and **He healed them**. 31 So the multitude marveled when they saw the mute speaking, the maimed made whole, the lame walking, and the blind seeing; and they glorified the God of Israel."*

19:1 *"Now it came to pass, when Jesus had finished these sayings, that He departed from Galilee and came to the region of Judea beyond the Jordan. 2 And great multitudes followed Him, and **He healed them there**."*

We have seen eight accounts in Matthew's gospel where all were healed. It is interesting to note that "eight" is the number of Christ, or Messiah; composed of 7, (which is the perfection of God) +1=8 therefore eight is perfection plus!

Most Christians live on second hand revelation. They only hear what teachers and preachers have to say and never go to God for themselves. This is a recipe for living in defeat. As a teacher of the word, I can only point you in the right direction. After that, it's up to you to dig for yourself and become established in the truth.

Let's go back to my time on the mountain that I spoke of, at the beginning of this chapter. The first scripture Jesus took me to that afternoon was Acts 10:38
"how God anointed Jesus of Nazareth with the Holy Spirit and with power, who went about doing good and healing all who were oppressed by the devil, for God was with Him."

23

Peter is the speaker here and he says that all the ones whom Jesus healed during His earthly ministry were oppressed by the devil.

My professor that I mentioned before had said that there were three reasons why people were sick. First: people were sick because of being attacked by the devil. Secondly: some were sick because God had allowed that sickness for a particular reason –perhaps to teach them something. And third: some were sick just because of natural causes, for instance they failed to eat right and take care of their body. But, Peter said that they were all oppressed by the devil, or perhaps there were some others but those Jesus had not healed, as if there were some made sick by God, He wouldn't have healed them.

Then he took me to Mat. 4:
Verse 23 and 24 say: *"Now Jesus went about all Galilee, teaching in their synagogues, preaching the gospel of the kingdom, and healing all kinds of sickness and all kinds of disease among the people. Then His fame went throughout all Syria; and they brought to Him all sick people who were afflicted with various diseases and torments, and those who were demon-possessed, epileptics, and paralytics; and He healed them."*

A WHOLE NATION HEALED
I was already somewhat familiar with this text but as I read over it again the words, "... **throughout all Syria**..." seemed to stand off the page at me. I suddenly realized something that I had not seen before. I knew that on this occasion Jesus had healed all the people in a particular place but I was not aware of the magnitude of what had happened. Syria is not a county or province like Galilee

24

but an actual nation that could have had a population of a few million people. Imagine an occurrence in your area. Imagine someone doing an evangelistic crusade in Vietnam near the Cambodian border and after a few days of preaching, rumors of the miracles that are taking place have circulated around the entire neighboring nation of Cambodia and every sick person in the entire country, every tormented person, every demon-possessed person, every epileptic, every paralytic person all are brought to the crusade and all of them are healed! What an event! I'm not sure how many people there were in Syria but there had to be at least two or three million. Both Syria and Cambodia look to be about the same size on the map. If half of them were sick (and that would be a conservative estimate) that would mean at least a million people plus the ones that helped, attended and carried them. There were no buses, trains or automobiles. They all walked or rode on a donkey to get there.

Anyway, what occurred to me right away was the following. If my professor was correct and some were sick because of being attacked by the devil, some were sick because God had allowed that sickness for a particular reason –perhaps to teach them something, then why were there none in the whole nation of Syria that God had made sick for some special reason? Did a few million Syrians have a special deal with God that allowed them a free pass? No, The Apostle Peter already told us that Jesus "*..went around doing good and healing all who were oppressed by the devil..*" These people didn't even know who God is, they were steeped in idolatry yet they were all healed. **This revelation shook me to the core. I couldn't get over it; a whole nation healed!**

From there he took me to other texts to cause me to understand how God teaches and trains his children. We will talk about this later.

This experience led me on a journey where I studied the entire Bible finding every occurrence of healing and miracles and trying to determine whether there was a pattern that would work today for receiving and ministering healing today. I started in the Gospels (Matthew, Mark, Luke and John) I looked very closely at the Life of Jesus and His traveling from place to place, preaching, teaching, healing and casting out demons. I discovered that about a fourth of the gospel record had to do with healing. I saw in the gospel of John that everything that Jesus said and did was the expressed will of His heavenly Father.

JESUS ALWAYS DID AND SPOKE THE WILL OF THE FATHER

You can search all the gospel narrative and you will not be able to find any place where Jesus refused to heal someone or inferred that it was the will of God for one to stay sick. Is it possible that Jesus acted in opposition to the will of His heavenly Father? This would be impossible because the scriptures plainly declare that everything He did and said was the will of God.

"He who sent Me is with Me. The Father has not left Me alone, for I always do those things that please Him." (Jn.8:29) and, again in verse 38 *"I speak what I have seen with My Father..."* Again in 5:19 & 30 Jesus declares, *"Most assuredly, I say to you, the Son can do nothing of Himself, but what He sees the Father do; for whatever He does, the Son also does in like manner...I can of Myself do nothing. As*

26

I hear, I judge; and My judgment is righteous, because I do not seek My own will but the will of the Father who sent Me."

So we see that there is absolutely no independent will, speech, or action between the Son and the Father. Therefore if Jesus during his earthly ministry healed all who came to Him in faith, then we can be assured that this was also the express will of the Father. Therefore, the answer to our question, **is it the will of God to heal all His children, is decidedly yes!**

CHAPTER THREE

THE CHARACTER AND NATURE OF GOD

Even among believers who know that God still heals today, there remains a prevalent concept that Jesus must be extremely busy running the universe and therefore my particular need must be of little consequence in the larger scheme of things and maybe He just doesn't have time to deal with my little problem. Some doubt His power but many doubt His willingness to heal.

What we need is to have our concept of God reformed by the scriptures.
Many believers have an erroneous concept of God that is out of line with God's own statements about Himself in the Bible. Many people, even Christians, feel that God must be mad at them most of the time. These people operate in a sin consciousness. Their own sin looms bigger in their own minds and hearts than the finished work of Christ. Regardless of how we feel or see ourselves we need to allow the Word of God to modify our thinking. We need to renew our minds by His word. God's word teaches us everything we need to know in order to have a correct understanding of who God is and His will for us in every circumstance of life.

The apostle Paul exhorts us in Romans 12:1
"I beseech you therefore, brethren, by the mercies of God, that you present your bodies a living sacrifice, holy, acceptable to God, which is your reasonable service. 2 And do not be conformed to this world, but be transformed by the renewing of your mind, that you may prove what is that good and acceptable and perfect will of God."

Most believers read their Bible and study a little scripture. Some are even accustomed to the activity of the Holy Spirit illuminating a word or a passage of scripture as they are reading, giving them insight into the particular passage. This is called revelation or openings of the scripture.

This activity of the Holy Spirit is actually not the goal but simply a signpost that says, "Dig here." If we will learn to sit quietly with the word it will ultimately change our relationship with God. Diligent meditation in God's word will change your thinking in any area that is out of agreement with God's thinking. We must learn to think like God thinks!

The Lord Himself said through Isaiah, *"For My thoughts are not your thoughts, nor are your ways My ways," says the LORD. "For as the heavens are higher than the earth, so are My ways higher than your ways, and My thoughts than your thoughts. For as the rain comes down, and the snow from heaven, and do not return there, but water the earth, and make it bring forth and bud, that it may give seed to the sower and bread to the eater, so shall My word be that goes forth from My mouth; it shall not return to Me void, but it shall accomplish what I please, and it shall prosper in the thing for which I sent it."* (55:8-11)

Many Christians believe that we can never understand God or learn to think like God thinks, but the Bible was written precisely for that reason; to teach us to think like God thinks. It is true that now, in our earthly existence, we certainly cannot know everything about God. All of eternity may not be sufficient to totally understand His magnificent greatness, but God has made available to us through the Bible all that we need to know in order to live holy and effective Christian lives.

The Apostle Peter tells us, "..*as His divine power has given to us all things that pertain to life and godliness, through the knowledge of Him who called us by glory and virtue, by which have been given to us exceedingly great and precious promises, that through these you may be partakers of the divine nature, having escaped the corruption that is in the world through lust.*" (2Pet. 1:3,4)

This process starts with understanding the character of God, understanding His love and mercy. He is not angry with you, He is not looking for an excuse to punish you. On the contrary, He is looking for a way to bless you! He is a God of love and compassion.

The apostle John said it like this, "*He who does not love does not know God, for God is love. In this the love of God was manifested toward us, that God has sent His only begotten Son into the world, that we might live through Him. In this is love, not that we loved God, but that He loved us and sent His Son to be the propitiation for our sins.*"
(1John 4:8-11)

Most of us would agree that there is nothing we can do to make God love us more, but at the same time there is nothing we can do to make God love us less. He is love, His very essence is love. He can do nothing outside of love. Look at the words of Jesus,

"*Or what man is there among you who, if his son asks for bread, will give him a stone? Or if he asks for a fish, will he give him a serpent? If you then, being evil, know how to give good gifts to your children, how much more will your Father who is in heaven give good things to those who ask Him!"* (Mat. 7:9-11)

Here Jesus speaks of God as a loving father who gives good things to his children. I have seen parents expend their entire savings and even mortgage their home to come up with the money to pay for expensive medical treatment or an operation, sometimes traveling to another country where medical treatment is more advanced, all this without really considering it a sacrifice. Why? Because of their love for a daughter or son. Yet, none would argue that their love for their own children was more perfect, pure, or selfless than God's love for them. How is it then that we doubt God's willingness to heal? We look at him as a stingy person who wouldn't give a cup of cold water to a person in need. Healing costs God neither time nor effort. *"Is anything too hard for the LORD?"* (GEN 18:14)

WHY DID JESUS HEAL?
Another common error is the idea that Jesus only healed in order to prove that He was the Son of God. Healing or doing miracles in itself did not prove that He was the Son of God. Abraham, Elijah, Elisha and others mentioned in the Old Testament healed people and even raised the dead, but none of them was the Son of God. , Samson performed miracles and lived in sin at the same time, so miracles are no proof in themselves of a special place with God or even being right with God. If Jesus healed only to prove that he possessed some special power He would have only needed to raise Lazarus from the dead. This would have been sufficient to prove His power.

The principle reasons for the healings and miracles that

Jesus did were:
(1) To demonstrate the arrival of the kingdom of God. (Luke 11:20)
(2) To fulfill the prophetic scriptures. (Mat.8:17) and
(3) Because he had compassion for the suffering people. (Mat.14:14; Mar.1:40)

(Not listed in order of importance.)

Actually, the miracles that Jesus performed were not accomplished by power that He had by reason of being the Son of God. All the miracles He did were done through the power that Jesus received from the Father, through the anointing of the Holy Spirit, as a prophet under the Abrahamic covenant ,the same as Elijah, Elisha and others mentioned previously. Understand, that we are not saying that Jesus was not the Son of God. He most surely was God made flesh, yet when He came to earth He laid down His divine nature and all the powers that came with it.
"...who, being in the form of God, did not consider it robbery to be equal with God, but made Himself of no reputation, taking the form of a servant, and coming in the likeness of men." (Phi. 2:6,7)

I remember hearing John Wimber (founder of the Vineyard Churches) say that in some of the stories of Jesus' healings we can pick up a sense of impatience and anger in Jesus, when He is dealing with the sick people. He is not angry at the people but at the work of the enemy and at the sickness itself. Jesus seems to be saying, "This is not right! This is out of line with my Father's will, and it must be stopped!" It becomes evident from these texts that sickness is a distortion or corruption of God's original plan.

Luke 12:11-16; John 11) It is evident from the number of instances quoted that the primary reason why Jesus healed so many people was because of His **great compassion**. Therefore, if Jesus healed during His earthly ministry because of His compassion, then we can be assured that He is still doing the same thing today, because Hebrews 13:8 plainly tells us; "Jesus Christ, the same yesterday, today, and forever." If Jesus healed because of His compassion and has stopped healing today, then the obvious conclusion is that His compassion has changed. The Bible teaches that God is love, (1Jn.4:7) Compassion is the outworking manifestation of love. Jesus' love could not change without His very inner nature changing. He, being God incarnate, cannot change! "For I am the LORD, I change not..." (Mal. 3:6)

Praise God for His unchanging nature, He is still in the healing business today, and will be until the end of the age.

CHAPTER FOUR

THE ORIGIN OF SICKNESS

Whatever theme we teach from the Bible, we need to analyze it in terms of several overarching biblical principles. One is the kingdom principle. We need to hold up whatever we are teaching and look at it through the lens of the kingdom of God, and see if it still holds up when measured against that understanding.

The kingdom of God is where everything is in God's order. There are three places in the Bible where the kingdom of God is perfectly established. They are: (1)The garden of Eden before the fall (2) The life of Jesus, and (3) Heaven. A thorough study of all the scriptures reveals that no sickness can be found in any of those three places. Therefore sickness cannot be considered to be part of God's kingdom and part of His plan and will for His children.

Jesus instructed His disciples to pray, " Your kingdom come, Your will be done on earth as it is in heaven." "On earth as it is in heaven.." What a powerful statement! Jesus is telling us that it is God's will for His heavenly will to be established on the earth.

Another could be called the Genesis or Eden principle. This is similar to the former, but often casts a different light on the subject. We need to look at healing in terms of what God did originally in Eden.

When we look at the subject of divine healing and

compare it to the basic understanding of the garden of Eden, we can find out several interesting facts. First, we see that there is no mention of sickness before the fall. We are told that everything God created was good, and the Old Testament tells us that sickness is an evil thing. (Gen.1:31; Deut. 7:15) Adam and Eve lived in a perfect world. They enjoyed divine health, abundance of all good things and peace. If they got hungry they simply reached up into a nearby tree and pulled down whatever fruit their heart desired. They had no knowledge [3]of anything evil. They did not know excessive hunger, thirst, cold, heat, or lack of anything, strife, fear, physical pain, or sickness. They lived in perfect harmony and communion with the Father God. Later when we find sickness mentioned, we find it in a list of things called evil or curses. (Deut.28:15-68)

God made a covenant with man, a covenant of dominion whereby man was to rule over all of the created order.

*"Then God said, "Let Us make man in Our image, according to Our likeness; let them have **dominion** over the fish of the sea, over the birds of the air, and over the cattle, over all the earth and over every creeping thing that creeps on the earth. So God created man in His own image; in the image of God He created him; male and female He created them. Then God blessed them, and God said to them, "Be fruitful and multiply; fill the earth and subdue it; **have dominion** over the fish of the sea, over the birds of the air, and over every living thing that moves on the earth." (Gen.1:26-28)*

---

[3]Knowledge in the biblical sense refers to intimacy; i.e. Gen.4:1 Now Adam knew Eve his wife, and she conceived and bore Cain..."

Notice that Man, (both Adam and Eve) were give dominion in three worlds, first over, "the fish of the sea," that's everything in the waters under the earth. Then, "..over the birds of the air.." That includes everything in the atmosphere over the earth. Then, "..and over the cattle.." That includes all that walks on the earth. Finally, included as a separate category, "...every creeping thing that creeps on the earth.." Creeping things in the literal Hebrew means things that glide swiftly over the ground. This obviously refers ahead to the being we will encounter in chap. 3, the serpent or the poisoner. This is where all the trouble starts.

> *"Now the serpent was more cunning than any beast of the field which the LORD God had made. And he said to the woman, 'Has God indeed said, You shall not eat of every tree of the garden?' And the woman said to the serpent, 'We may eat the fruit of the trees of the garden; but of the fruit of the tree which is in the midst of the garden, God has said, 'You shall not eat it, nor shall you touch it, lest you die.' And the serpent said to the woman, 'You will not surely die. For God knows that in the day you eat of it your eyes will be opened, and you will be like God, knowing good and evil.' So when the woman saw that the tree was good for food, that it was pleasant to the eyes, and a tree desirable to make to make one wise, she took of its fruit and ate. She also gave to her husband with her, and he ate. Then the eyes of both of them were opened..." (Gen.3:1-7)*

The standard rules of biblical interpretation require that we interpret any text literally, unless the context requires otherwise. In other words, if a literal interpretation seems so absurd that it couldn't possibly be accepted literally or if a literal interpretation would contradict the plain, simple to understand texts especially in the New Testament, then we should look for an alternate meaning. To some commentators a talking snake is too absurd, for others it's not. My sense is that it could be both. We can accept the possibility of a literal interpretation and, at the same time, see within it a story that goes beyond the literal meaning. Whether or not Eve saw a literal snake talking to her is irrelevant. The snake represents Satan in a symbolic form and teaches us his strategies and method to lead man into temptation, sin and death.

WHO IS SATAN?

Who is this serpent or the poisoner?

If we put together all the biblical text that has to do with Satan we see an interesting picture emerge. Two texts, in particular, give us special insight into the character and nature of Satan. Those are Ezekiel 28:13-18; and Isaiah 14:12-17.

In the beginning of Ezekiel 28, we find a prophetic word concerning the Prince of Tyre. There is nothing in the first few verses to lead us to believe that the author is referring to anyone more than a human ruler. Then in verse twelve, the prophet speaks to the King of Tyre and the direction changes. Soon we see that he is no longer referring to a human ruler but someone of supernatural character. Let's look at the text.

"Son of man, take up a lamentation for the king of Tyre, and say to him, Thus says the Lord God: You were the seal of perfection, full of wisdom and perfect in beauty. 13 You were in Eden, the garden of God; every precious stone was

your covering: the Sardis, topaz, and diamond, beryl, onyx, and jasper, sapphire, turquoise, and emerald with gold. The workmanship of your timbrels and pipes [4] was prepared for you on the day you were created. 14 You were the anointed cherub who covers; I established you; you were on the holy mountain of God; you walked back and forth in the midst of fiery stones. 15 You were perfect in your ways from the day you were created, till iniquity was found in you. 16 By the abundance of your trading you became filled with violence within, and you sinned; therefore I cast you as a profane thing out of the mountain of God; and I destroyed you, O covering cherub, from the midst of the fiery stones. 17 Your heart was lifted up because of your beauty; you corrupted your wisdom for the sake of your splendor; I cast you to the ground, I laid you before kings, that they might gaze at you. 18 You defiled your sanctuaries by the multitude of your iniquities, by the iniquity of your trading; therefore I brought fire from your midst; it devoured you, and I turned you to ashes upon the earth in the sight of all who saw you. 19 All who knew you among the peoples are astonished at you; you have become a horror, and shall be no more forever." (28:12-19)

First we see that this being was in Eden. The only humans in Eden were Adam and Eve. Then we also see that he was created by God, and is called the covering cherub. A cherub is, in Hebrew understanding; beings of sublime and celestial nature and of amazing power, not little children with wings coming out of their shoulders, as is often depicted in popular art work. This covering cherub

---

[4]. The words timbrels and pipes in Hebrew; *mela'kah* and *toph* have a more direct reference to a bezel or settings for precious stones, rather than to musical instruments.

is anointed to protect and cover, thus an angel of great authority. This angel becomes corrupted because of his beauty, his wisdom becomes corrupted and he is cast out of heaven. It would be difficult to imagine that the prophet might be speaking of anyone but Satan himself.

Then in Isaiah we find further information.
14:12-19; *"How you are fallen from heaven, O Lucifer, son of the morning! How you are cut down to the ground, you who weakened the nations! 13 For you have said in your heart: 'I will ascend into heaven, I will exalt my throne above the stars of God; I will also sit on the mount of the congregation on the farthest sides of the north; 14 I will ascend above the heights of the clouds, I will be like the Most High.' 15 Yet you shall be brought down to Sheol, to the lowest depths of the Pit. 16 Those who see you will gaze at you, and consider you, saying: 'Is this the man who made the earth tremble, who shook kingdoms, 17 who made the world as a wilderness and destroyed its cities, who did not open the house of his prisoners?'18 All the kings of the nations, all of them, sleep in glory, everyone in his own house; 19 but you are cast out of your grave like an abominable branch, Like the garment of those who are slain, thrust through with a sword, who go down to the stones of the pit, like a corpse trodden under foot."*

This passage refers specifically to Lucifer or "The light bringer" which was Satan's name before his fall. It tells of his attempt to raise himself up to be even more powerful than Yahweh himself and of his immediate failure and expulsion from heaven. Note that five times Satan rises up and declares his rebellion, exalting his own will against that of God himself concluding with the phrase, *"...I will be like the most high."* Does that sound familiar? Of course, that's exactly what he used later to tempt Eve with. *"For God knows that in the day you eat of it your eyes will be opened, and you will be like God, knowing good and evil."* (Gen.3:5)

Many commentators agree that Satan convinced a third of the angels to enter into rebellion with him against God, although this is not plainly supported by scripture it is suggested in Jude 1:6 and Revelations 12, where he is called the dragon. Most Bible scholars believe that this group of fallen angels actually were cast down to the earth and became the demons. Others believe that the demons are the spirits of a race of men who were destroyed before the creation of Adam, or from the fornication of angels with men. None of these theories are relevant to our study however interesting they might be. All we need to know is that Satan and demons really exist. They are spirit beings and therefore are invisible to the human eye, but that does not mean that they don't have power. Many Christians today view Satan and demons as figments of archaic mythology, they believe that they are just principles of evil, not actual beings but, rest assured, that they are quite real and they have power.

HOW POWERFUL IS THE DEVIL?
Satan is a being of considerable but limited power and authority, but he is a being created by God and no match for God in power. Christians generally fall into two categories concerning what they think about Satan. It seems that about half of them think the devil is almost as powerful as God and that God will win out in the end but just by a hair. The others believe that the devil has almost

no influence at all and that everything that happens in the earth is the perfect will of God. Both these views are in error and the truth lies somewhere in between the two extreme views. Isaiah testifies of Satan's power being enough to destroy cities, and to twist the very creation of God. "Is this the man who made the earth tremble, who shook kingdoms, who made the world as a wilderness and destroyed its cities.." .(Isa.14:16-17) Yet Satan and demons are created beings with limited power. They can do no creative miracle, and are extremely limited in the supernatural. I have often been asked how witchdoctors and shaman do their healing. The only diseases that they can heal are diseases that are caused directly by evil spirits. They conjure a stronger spirit than the one that is causing the sickness, who in turn extracts the weaker demon. The problem is that the stronger demon, having gained entry in the person, is allowed to take over. The person is usually relived of the original sickness but worse things begin to happen because of the presence of the stronger demon. Some people after having received Christ as savior continue to resort to witchdoctors and those who affect magical cures for healing without realizing that they are opening themselves up to demon infestation.

IS SATAN THE AUTHOR OF SICKNESS?
Let's look at the New Testament. First in Luke 13:10-17; Please, turn in your Bible to this passage and read it carefully before proceeding any further. Here we find a story of a woman bent over double that could not raise herself up. Jesus says that it was a "spirit of infirmity" that caused this sickness. Later in verse 16 he says, "So ought not this woman, being a daughter of Abraham, **whom Satan has bound** - think of it - for eighteen years, be

41

loosed from this bond on the Sabbath?" Jesus here brings forth two reasons why this woman had a right to be healed even on the Sabbath, which was the holy day of the Jews in which no one was supposed to work. First he said she is a daughter of Abraham and secondly he says that Satan had bound her. Satan was responsible for her malady. Of course this does not prove more than one case, so let's use scripture to interpret scripture and continue to look at related texts.

Remember that we already looked at Acts 10:38; where Peter was preaching in the home of an Italian military man and in the midst of his sermon makes this statement. *"how God anointed Jesus of Nazareth with the Holy Spirit and with power, who went about doing good and **healing all who were oppressed by the devil,** for God was with Him."* The apostle Peter is speaking here and he tells us that Jesus, in His earthly ministry, healed **only those who were oppressed by the devil.** Therefore, if there were any, who were made sick by "God" in any of Jesus' meetings, He did not heal any of them. In the next chapter, we go into greater depth concerning the author of sickness, further proving that sickness does not come from God.

CHAPTER FIVE
HEALING: PROMISED IN BOTH OLD AND NEW COVENANT

Let's return to the text that we noted in the last chapter from Luke13:10-16.

Now He was teaching in one of the synagogues on the Sabbath.11 And behold, there was a woman who had a spirit of infirmity eighteen years, and was bent over and could in no way raise herself up. 12 But when Jesus saw her, He called her to Him and said to her, "Woman, you are loosed from your infirmity." 13:13 And He laid His hands on her, and immediately she was made straight, and glorified God.

14 But the ruler of the synagogue answered with indignation, because Jesus had healed on the Sabbath; and he said to the crowd, "There are six days on which men ought to work; therefore come and be healed on them, and not on the Sabbath day." 15 The Lord then answered him and said, "Hypocrite! Does not each one of you on the Sabbath loose his ox or his donkey from the stall, and lead it away to water it? 16 "So ought not this woman, being a daughter of Abraham, whom Satan has bound - think of it - for eighteen years, be loosed from this bond on the Sabbath?"

We considered verse 16 there, in particular, the statement "whom Satan has bound - think of it - for eighteen years," deciding that Satan was indeed, responsible, either directly or indirectly, for all sickness. Now we want to look at the first part of verse 16 and pay close attention to another part of the same statement. Jesus referred to this woman as a daughter of Abraham,

43

v-16   "*So ought not this woman, being a daughter of Abraham...be loosed from this bond on the Sabbath?*" Jesus could easily have referred to this woman simply as, "this woman..." or in some other manner, but He, on purpose said, "**daughter of Abraham**." I believe Jesus said this to call our attention to something in particular, namely, this woman's ancestry. She was a Jewess, an inheritor of the covenant of Abraham.

We need to take a few moments here and establish what a covenant is, for there are many believers that don't know. In modern times we don't understand solemn agreements. We make contract in business and make promises in our social life. But, few of us take our word very seriously. Perhaps, the closest thing we can find in modern culture that compares to a covenant is the marriage ceremony. In it, solemn vows are made and generally expected to be kept. In ancient times men made covenants sealed in blood. Two men might make a covenant because of a strong bond of friendship, agreeing to protect each other, to provide what one might need. An example of this is Jonathan and David. Two families, or smaller tribes, might enter into a covenant of blood in order to protect themselves from a stronger tribe or just to insure that there would not be war between the two. An example Abraham and Abimelech, (Gen.21:27)
In the formation of a covenantial agreement five things are generally considered.
1. The power, ability, character of the other party. (is he worthy of trust?)
2. The strength of the vows, (where do I fit in to this thing?)
3. The vows as such. (What is expected of me, is it a good deal?)

4. The blessing (if I obey) and the curse (if I disobey)
5. Inheritance, (Does this agreement have a future)

These five factors will be found in almost every covenant mentioned in the Bible. The ancient peoples, especially tribal people, were careful to keep all covenant vows. A person who broke covenant would often be killed by his own family. Yet ,it was almost unheard of. The Bible itself is based on the concept of covenant. The writings themselves are the terms and statutes of God's covenant with His children. Therefore, God is bound by His own decree to fulfill all His word in the lives of those who live in obedience to His statutes. Healing is part of God's covenant, both in the Old Covenant and the New Covenant.

Therefore, we see that, when Jesus referred to the woman as a "**daughter of Abraham**", He was calling her and our attention to the fact that she was an inheritor of the covenant of Abraham. His tone and manner are made obvious by His words. He is irritated by the fact that she is even sick, not irritated at her but at the enemy for attacking her, and even more by the opposition of the Pharisees, as they are preventing the will of God from taking place in her life.

Now we will explore some of the particular promises of the covenant of Abraham, (the Old Testament)

GEN 20:17 *So Abraham prayed to God; and God healed Abimelech, his wife, and his maidservants. Then they bore children; 18 for the LORD had closed up all the wombs of the house of Abimelech because of Sarah, Abraham's wife.*

45

There is another principle of Bible interpretation that is called the principle of" first mention" That says; the first place in the Bible where a subject is mentioned often reveals special truth concerning the subject. In the above text, which is the first place where healing is mentioned, we find that it is granted by God in response to the prayer of a believer, in this case for a pagan king.

EXO 15:26 "..*If you diligently heed the voice of the LORD your God and do what is right in His sight, give ear to His commandments and keep all His statutes, I will put none of the diseases on you which I have brought on the Egyptians.* **For I am the LORD who heals you.**"

This is one of the most commonly known promises because the Hebrew text contains the redemptive name **Yahweh-Rapha** – Yahweh the healer or doctor. Notice He says **I am**, not I was or will be. The very name Yahweh means 'I am' because He is always now He is the unchanging God, the same yesterday today and forever! (Heb.13:8)

EXO 23:25 *"So you shall serve the LORD your God, and He will bless your bread and your water. And I will take sickness away from the midst of you. 26; "No one shall suffer miscarriage or be barren in your land; I will fulfill the number of your days."*

This is one of my favorite healing promises in the Bible, for two reasons. First: because of the blessing on our food and water. I often travel into remote regions of different countries to preach the gospel. Sometimes the water is contaminated and often I end up eating strange things that people give me to eat, but I've never gotten parasites and/ or food poisoning. I think only twice in twenty years of travel have I gotten any adverse reaction from anything I ate, and those didn't last long. I praise God for His covenant of protection.

Secondly: because of the promise to married couples of having children. I have prayed for dozens of different couples who have been married up to ten years without children and told them to meditate on this promise and others. Generally within only a few days they were pregnant. If this is your situation, search out the numerous promises concerning this situation and appropriate them for yourselves.

DEU 7:12-15; *"Then it shall come to pass, because you listen to these judgments, and keep and do them, that the LORD your God will keep with you the covenant and the mercy which He swore to your fathers. 13 "And He will love you and bless you and multiply you; He will also bless the fruit of your womb and the fruit of your land, your grain and your new wine and your oil, the increase of your cattle and the offspring of your flock, in the land of which He swore to your fathers to give you. 14 "You shall be blessed above all peoples; there shall not be a male or female barren among you or among your livestock. 15 "**And the LORD will take away from you all sickness**, and will afflict you with none of the terrible diseases of Egypt which you have known, but will lay them on all those who hate you."*

This is one of the first comprehensive, Old Testament promises which includes healing from all sickness. Some say that this is not of the Abrahamic covenant , but notice the wording of verse twelve "... the LORD your God will keep with you the covenant and the mercy **which He**

swore to your fathers." Who were the fathers? Obviously, it was Abraham, Isaac, and Jacob who were the fathers of the nation of Israel. Therefore these promises were initially given to Abraham, and they were good **for the woman of Luke 13.**

HEALING IN THE PSALMS & PROVERBS

Psalm 103:1 *"Bless the LORD, O my soul; And all that is within me, bless His holy name!2 Bless the LORD, O my soul, And forget not all His benefits:3 Who forgives all your iniquities,* **Who heals all your diseases,***4 Who redeems your life from destruction, Who crowns you with loving kindness and tender mercies,5 Who satisfies your mouth with good things, So that your youth is renewed like the eagle's."*

Psalm 107:20 *"He sent His word and* **healed** *them, And delivered them from their destructions."*

Prov. 4:20-22; *"My son, give attention to my words; incline your ear to my sayings. Do not let them depart from your eyes; keep them in the midst of your heart; For they are life to those who find them, and* **health to all their flesh.***
Keep your heart with all diligence, for out of it spring the issues of life."*

Psalms 107:20, and Prov.4:20-22; give God's recipe for healing, **the medicine of His word.** We must pay attention to it, obey it, constantly be meditating on it. That is what will produce the desired result in our lives.

THE INTERPETATION OF TYPES AND SYMBOLS

The Bible contains a wealth of different figures of speech and uses symbols and types, to aid in a complete understanding of God's truth. Symbols are emblems or signs that represent something other than themselves. The Bible contains symbolic colors, numbers, creatures, gestures, rituals and so forth. Some examples of biblical symbols are; the color purple representing royalty, the number seven representing the perfection of God and the serpent representing Satan.

Types are like symbols but are always futuristic. Thus, all the feasts of the Hebrew people are types of future redemption and of different aspects of the life and ministry of Jesus the Messiah.

Some care must be exercised in the study of types and symbols. Some Church movements tend to build most of their teaching on Old Testament types and symbols. What we believe and teach should never be based on types and symbols. We should always establish what we believe on clear New Testament passages. We can however, use biblical types and symbols to support what we teach or as teaching examples because they are easy to remember. Also we should only use types and symbols that are clearly supported by the weight of Scripture. If there is no clear biblical evidence for the use of a symbol then we should refrain from using them.

THE TYPE OF THE BRONZE SERPENT

The passage below uses one of the classic types of redemption which demonstrates clearly that healing is part of our redemption.

NUM 21:7-9 *"Therefore the people came to Moses, and said, "We have sinned, for we have spoken against the LORD and against you; pray to the LORD that He take away the serpents from us." So Moses prayed for the people. 8 Then the LORD said to Moses, "Make a bronze serpent, and set it on a pole; and it shall be that everyone who is bitten, when he looks at it, shall live. 9 So Moses made a bronze serpent, and put it on a pole; and so it was, if a serpent had bitten anyone, when he looked at the bronze serpent, he lived."*

The serpent represents Satan who was rendered powerless against the believer by **the crucifixion of the man, Christ Jesus.** As the writer of Hebrews says,

"Inasmuch then as the children have partaken of flesh and blood, He Himself likewise shared in the same, that through death He might destroy [5] him who had the power of death, that is, the devil, and release those who through fear of death were all their lifetime subject to bondage." (2:14,15.)

Thus, the Israelites were healed by gazing intently at the bronze serpent nailed on a pole. This looks forward to the destruction of Satan's power by Jesus Christ. The serpent also represents the satanic nature in man, which received a deathblow at the cross. We look to the New Testament to find the explanation of this type and find it clearly portrayed in JOH 3:14-17. Most of us know verse 16 by

---

[5] The word destroy here is *katargeo*, acc. Strong; "to render idle, unemployed, inactivate, inoperative, to cause a person or thing to have no further efficiency, to deprive of force, influence, power." It is obvious that Satan's power is not completely destroyed, but it is impossible for it to triumph over the power of the gospel.

heart, but few have any understanding of the context which points back to the Old Testament.

"And as Moses lifted up the serpent in the wilderness, even so must the Son of Man be lifted up,[6] that whoever believes in Him should not perish but have eternal life. For God so loved the world that He gave His only begotten Son, that whoever believes in Him should not perish but have everlasting life. For God did not send His Son into the world to condemn the world, but that the world through Him might be saved."

Therefore, we see that the sacrifice of the Son of God is typified in the Old Testament, as not only the answer for sin, but the answer for sickness. We will see more about the relation between sin and sickness later.

---

[6] The term "lifted up" does not mean glorified as is commonly thought, but is a common Greek figure of speech for crucifixion, which was the common form of execution at that time.

CHAPTER SIX

HEALING PROVIDED THROUGH CHRIST'S SUFFERING

Normally this subject would be entitled, "Healing in the atonement," but since we believe that atonement is an Old Testament concept, we have therefore chosen another title. Atonement means "covering" . A large portion of the prophetic scriptures concerning the Messiah are found in Isaiah. This one speaks specifically of Christ's suffering and physical healing, as well as forgiveness of sins.

"Who has believed our message and to whom has the arm of the LORD been revealed? 2 He grew up before him like a tender shoot, and like a root out of dry ground. He had no beauty or majesty to attract us to him, nothing in his appearance that we should desire him. 3 He was despised and rejected by men, a man of sorrows, and familiar with suffering. Like one from whom men hide their faces he was despised, and we esteemed him not. 4 Surely he took up our **sicknesses** *and carried our* **pains***, yet we considered him stricken by God, smitten by him, and afflicted. 5 But he was pierced for our transgressions, he was crushed for our iniquities; the punishment that brought us peace was upon him, and by his wounds we are healed."* (Isaiah 53:1-5 NIV)

Many translations weaken the impact of verse four by the translation of the words *sickness* and *pains* as *griefs* and *sorrows*. The word translated sickness in the NIV here is," *choloy"*. In Hebrew, it appears nineteen times besides this passage. It is used fourteen times in passages directly relating to physical sickness, one time referring to physical injury from a fall and four times referring symbolically to Israel's sick condition but never refers to something that could be considered "grief." The second word, pain, *makob* in Hebrew, is a much more general term. It means, pain, in the general sense. Some commentators who don't believe in healing, attempt to explain away this clear passage as referring only to spiritual infirmity or grief. The general usage and clear meaning, dictate otherwise. There are also five different specific terms that the writer could have chosen which refer only to grief or mental anguish and are never used to speak of physical sickness. This prophesy, given over 500 years before Jesus birth, gives plain evidence, that the sacrifice of Christ, paid the full price, for not only our sins, but also for our diseases and pains.

J. Alec Motyer, an evangelical theologian, in his commentary on the prophet Isaiah says,
"Whatever people may have thought about the sorrows and sufferings they saw, the truth was dramatically different. 'He' is an emphatic pronoun. (*Vnasa'*) means to lift up (off of someone, in this case.) And *'carried'* is to take as one's own burden. And 'infirmities', translated 'suffering' in v.3b is the weakness of sickness, which coupled with sorrows, encapsulates all that mars our lives." [7]

Evangelical tradition holds to a limited atonement that only covers for "spiritual suffering" not physical. Motyer violates that traditional interpretation with his statement and truly represents what the prophet is saying.
The final phrase, "..by his wounds we are healed." Is the climax of the whole prophesy. 'Are' is in the Heb. Actually

---

[7] Motyer; Isaiah; p.430

should be 'were'—past tense. The prophet looks into the future where Messiah pays the full price for all those who believe and sees it as already done. God's time dimension sees future occurrences and treats them as fact. As Yahweh releases truth to the heart of the prophet and the prophet speaks it out, for God, it is already done, it is unchangeable reality. *'Pierced' in v.5 (Hall)* is found in Isaiah only in (51:9) where it is used of the death wound to the Dragon.[8] It usually means to 'pierce fatally' (Job. 26:13; Ps. 109:22)

"Awake, awake! Clothe yourself with strength, O arm of the LORD; awake, as in days gone by, as in generations of old. Was it not you who cut Rahab (Egypt) *to pieces, who pierced that monster* (dragon) *through? 10 Was it not you who dried up the sea, the waters of the great deep, who made a road in the depths of the sea so that the redeemed might cross over? 11 The ransomed of the LORD will return. They will enter Zion with singing; everlasting joy will crown their heads. Gladness and joy will overtake them, and sorrow and sighing will flee away."* (Isaiah 51:9-11)

Note that Messiah is called "the arm of the Lord" in (53:1) and He is pierced through for our transgressions, and previously (51:9) He is the one who pierces the dragon, the source of sin and sickness. The final result of the prophecy is the full manifestation of kingdom reality, the new exodus, paradise restored. First, a highway is provided for the redeemed to cross over, and the ransomed of the Lord return, they enter Zion with singing, and with everlasting joy crowning their heads.

---

[8] tanniyn, a marine or land monster, snake

What an amazing poetic description of the final consummation of our redemption, spoken by Isaiah! Our redemption, not only includes forgiveness of sin, healing for our bodies, peace for our minds but also the healing of the land itself. All of it comes through the suffering of the servant—Messiah, Christ Jesus himself.

So we see that healing is not just part, of the birthright of New Testament believers but actually, the entire Old Testament contains numerous promises of healing. True followers of God in Old Testament times could appropriate healing through the promises and trust God for full healing. That's why Jesus could say to the woman in Luke thirteen, "you are loosed from your infirmity." even though Jesus had not yet been to the cross, He saw the work as already finished therefore He spoke to the woman who was bent over double and not able to raise herself up, in the present tense, as if she was already healed "..you are loosed..."
And the word says, "immediately she was made straight and glorified God."

Isaiah's statement is quoted again in part, in two places in the New Testament.
MAT 8:16,17; *When evening had come, they brought to Him many who were demon-possessed. And He cast out the spirits with a word, and healed all who were sick, 17 that it might be fulfilled which was spoken by Isaiah the prophet, saying: "He Himself took our infirmities and bore our sicknesses."*

1PE 2:24 *who Himself bore our sins in His own body on the tree, that we, having died to sins, might live for righteousness - by whose stripes you were healed.*

Jesus has paid the price for you as well, take a hold of His promises of healing, because it is for you now. Accept it as fact and allow the Holy Spirit to operate in your body until it is fully manifested.

CHAPTER SEVEN

STUMBLING BLOCKS TO HEALING

There are several passages of scripture that opponents of healing grab a hold of, in order to negate any positive message of healing. One of these passages is concerning what is called, " Paul's thorn in the flesh."

When I was a very young believer, we were attending a small community church in the village where we lived. My wife and I attended a conference in another town, where there was several sessions on healing. When we returned home and attended Church the following Sunday, I was talking with the pastor after the meeting and he complained that he didn't feel well. Emboldened by the teaching I had heard, I offered to pray for him. The pastor politely declined saying that there were just some things that a young Christian like me would not understand. As I questioned him on the subject, he claimed that there were some people that God had appointed to suffer, like Paul, for instance, who God gave a thorn in the flesh and refused to remove it even though Paul prayed earnestly three times. I had just heard a whole teaching that covered Paul's thorn, Job's situation and other obstacles to healing. I answered the pastor according to what I had learned. He was speechless having no reply but was obviously not receptive to my argument. I learned later that simply having scripture and logic on your side may win the argument but does not necessarily win people over to your point of view or help them.

Let's look closely at this issue since Satan has convinced

many, especially ministers of the gospel that the reason they suffer with sickness is that they too have been given a "thorn in the flesh."

PAUL'S THORN
2Cor.12:7-10; *And lest I should be exalted above measure by the abundance of the revelations, a thorn in the flesh was given to me, a* <u>messenger of Satan</u> *to buffet me, lest I be exalted above measure. 8 Concerning this thing I pleaded with the Lord three times that it might depart from me. 9 And He said to me, "My grace is sufficient for you, for My strength is made perfect in weakness." Therefore most gladly I will rather boast in my infirmities, that the power of Christ may rest upon me. 10 Therefore I take pleasure in infirmities, [weakness] in reproaches, in needs, in persecutions, in distresses, for Christ's sake. For when I am weak, then I am strong.*

The assumption here is that this: "Thorn in the flesh," refers to some sort of physical ailment. Some translations even say "a painful physical ailment" a totally erroneous translation. Some say that Paul suffered with a painful eye disease, others with a bad back and numerous other ideas are put forward by commentators and preachers. But, what does the text actually say? Does it say that Paul suffered with a painful physical ailment that God refused to heal? Let's look closely at the text. The first key word here is the word "messenger" which was translated from the Greek word, *aggelos*. The word is translated 174 times as *angel* and as *messenger* 6 times. Three references where it is translated, *messenger,* it refers to John the Baptist, one to John's disciples, once to Jesus' disciples. Once it is translated, spies", referring to the spies that Joshua sent to Jericho. In every one of these uses of,

58

aggelos ,the word refers to angels, people or demons, not to diseases, conditions or situations.

The apostle Paul, as a trained Jewish Rabbi, had large portions of the Torah (Old Testament) committed to memory. He often used words that connect the thinking of any first century Jewish student of the scriptures with a portion or sense of the Old Testament theology. In the passage we are considering, Paul also uses the word " thorn". Let's look at the Old Testament again and determine if there is a connection.

Here, in Numbers 33:55, God himself is speaking, *"But if you do not drive out the inhabitants of the land from before you, then it shall be that those whom you let remain shall be irritants in your eyes and **thorns in your sides**, and they shall harass you in the land where you dwell."*

Joshua 23:13 *"know for certain that the LORD your God will no longer drive out these nations from before you. But they shall be snares and traps to you, and scourges on your sides and **thorns** in your eyes, until you perish from this good land which the LORD your God has given you."*

Every time the word "thorn" is used in the OT. symbolically ,it refers to people. Therefore, it is simply poor Bible interpretation to take these common usages of different Greek or Hebrew words and assume that they refer to something totally different than the common rabbinic usage.

The use of *aggelos* as messenger and thorn(s) speaks clearly to us that the situation Paul was dealing with, had to do with people. If one studies Paul's life as recorded in

Acts and his own statements about his life, this fact is confirmed. Let's look at one example.

2CO 11:22-30; *"Are they Hebrews? So am I. Are they Israelites? So am I. Are they Abraham's descendants? So am I. 23 Are they servants of Christ? (I am out of my mind to talk like this.) I am more. I have worked much harder, been in prison more frequently, been flogged more severely, and been exposed to death again and again. 24 Five times I received from the Jews the forty lashes minus one. 25 Three times I was beaten with rods, once I was stoned, three times I was ship-wrecked, I spent a night and a day in the open sea, 26 I have been constantly on the move. I have been in danger from rivers, in danger from bandits, in danger from my own countrymen, in danger from Gentiles; in danger in the city, in danger in the country, in danger at sea; and in danger from false brothers. 27 I have labored and toiled and have often gone without sleep; I have known hunger and thirst and have often gone without food; I have been cold and naked. 28 Besides everything else, I face daily the pressure of my concern for all the churches. 29 Who is weak, and I do not feel weak? Who is led into sin, and I do not inwardly burn? 30 If I must boast, I will boast of the things that show my weakness."*

If sickness was Paul's lot in life, along with all the other things that he suffered, then he should have included it in this comprehensive list of twenty-eight things that he suffered in his ministry. Any open-minded Bible student can read carefully through the Acts and find that the trial that Paul was experiencing in his flesh when he preached the gospel for the first time in Galatia was not caused by some disease of the eyes but by being stoned until he was thought to be dead.

(Gal.4:13-15)

Paul affirms to us over and over again that we have no biblical promise of deliverance from tribulation and persecution until the age to come but he does affirm that we have the promise of healing and health.

Acts14:22   "We must through many tribulations enter the kingdom of God."
2Tim 3: 12 "Yes, and all who desire to live godly in Christ Jesus will suffer persecution."

WHAT ABOUT JOB?

Another favorite scripture of those who want to discount healing entirely or to make it a rarity—something that God only does occasionally, is the problem of Job. They say, "Yes, but what about Job?" He suffered with a painful ailment all his life and was never delivered." Let's look at the book of Job and see if we can determine if this thought is true.

Remember, as we look at Job, that the story is believed to be one of the oldest in the Bible. It is also one of the most difficult and mysterious texts in the biblical record. If we follow clear and agreed upon principles of Bible interpretation we must not use Old Testament scriptures to interpret the New Testament and we must not use difficult and mysterious texts to interpret clear and direct statements of Jesus, Paul and the other New Testament writers. This does not mean, however, that we ignore difficult books, like Job, but that we try to interpret them in their place, submitted under New Testament truth. If we did not apply these principles of interpretation, we would be sacrificing our calves and lambs to God and circumcising our boys on the eighth day.

First, the text tells us that (1) Job was very rich (2) that his sons spent a lot of time dedicated to eating, drinking and partying (3) that Job made regular burnt offerings for his children. Then the scene switches to heaven and we see that the "sons of God" came before God's throne to present themselves. The term "sons of God" refers to the heavenly beings, among whom Satan originally was a part.[9] The story continues to explain that Yahweh, for reasons that remain unexplained, permitted Satan first, to attack Job's goods and his family and later to attack his body but not to take his life. Raiding bands first killed his servants and stole his crops from his barns and then, lightning strikes killed his livestock. Finally, a windstorm like a tornado came and killed his children who were busy partying at one of their houses. Job's response is: *"Then Job arose and tore his robe and shaved his head, and he fell to the ground and worshiped. And he said: 'Naked I came from my mother's womb, and naked shall I return there. The LORD gave, and the LORD has taken away; blessed be the name of the LORD.'"* (1:20,21)

It is evident from the context that Job is mistaken. It was the LORD that gave but it was Satan, not the Lord who took away. None the less, Job remained innocent before

---

[9] According to Delitzsch this refers to the holy ones, and is the assembly of the heavenly spirits, from which, as angels of God, they go forth into the universe and among men. It is also further the teaching of Scripture, that one of these spirits has withdrawn himself from the love of God, has reversed the truth of his bright existence, and in sullen ardent self-love is become the enemy of God, and everything godlike in the creation.

God, since he only lacked revelation of who was responsible for his problems.

The fact that Job was incorrect in his appraisal of the situation has not prevented multitudes of pastors and ministers from using this text at funeral services, thus blaming God for the death of a loved one. It is time that preachers place the blame squarely upon the real culprit, Satan! Satan is the destroyer. He was responsible for the lightning strikes, the tornado, and the raiding bands as well as Job's sickness. The fact remains, however, that somehow, Satan gained access to Job's life, the hedge that God had built around Job had been torn down.

Later Satan is able to afflict Job physically as well.

"Then Satan went forth from the presence of Jehovah, and smote Job with sore boils, from the sole of his foot to his crown." (2:7)

On top of this Job's wife tempts him to turn away from God. 9 She says, *"Do you still hold to your integrity? Curse God and die!"* At this point Job holds fast to his integrity, and he says to her, *"You speak as one of the foolish women speaks. Shall we indeed accept good from God, and shall we not accept adversity?"* Later Job's three friends come to console him but actually they participate in his further suffering and affliction by bringing a lying accusation against him that he has sinned in some way to cause the evil to come into his life.

WHY WAS JOB AFFLICTED?
The only explanation that appears in the text is that Job lived in fear that these things would take place.
"For the thing I greatly feared has come upon me, and what I dreaded has happened to me." (3:25) Fear is an opposite of the force of faith and this fear could have

caused his hedge of protection to be removed. Still, we are faced with the mystery of why God needed to point out to Satan the fact that Job's hedge had been removed.

RESISTING THE DEVIL
The New Testament tells us, "*Be sober, be vigilant; because your adversary the devil walks about like a roaring lion, seeking whom he may devour. Resist him, steadfast in the faith, knowing that the same sufferings are experienced by your brotherhood in the world.*" (1Peter 5:8,9) and Ephesians 6:16; "*above all, taking the shield of faith with which you will be able to quench all the fiery darts of the wicked one.*"

We, as believers, are called to resist Satan in the faith, or with the shield of faith, which will quench all of his fiery darts. It seems that Job threw away his confidence. He never turned his back on God but he lamented the day he was born and wished he could die. (3:3 ff.) We remember that Job had little or no revelation on the existence or operation of Satan and demons and was not responsible for that which he did not know. Also, we must affirm that the Bible mentions Job as one of the most righteous men that ever lived.

JOB'S FINAL RESTORATION
Finally we see that those who say that Job suffered his entire life in this condition are greatly mistaken. It seems that many have never bothered to read completely through to the end of the story, "*And the LORD restored Job's losses when he prayed for his friends. Indeed the LORD gave Job twice as much as he had before...Now the LORD blessed the latter days of Job more than his beginning; for he had fourteen thousand sheep, six thousand camels, one*

*thousand yoke of oxen, and one thousand female donkeys.
He also had seven sons and three daughters."* (42:10-13)

So we see that regardless of what caused these events, the
Lord restored to Job all that he had lost and blessed him
beyond measure. Hebrew scholars who have spent time
in this difficult book believe that the entire time frame of
the book is less than one year, so it wasn't the endless
suffering that some suppose.

THE MAN BORN BLIND

Another passage that is commonly used by opponents of
healing is the story of the man born blind found in John
Chapter Nine.

*"Now as Jesus passed by, He saw a man who was blind from
birth. 2 And His disciples asked Him, saying, 'Rabbi, who
sinned, this man or his parents, that he was born blind?' 3
Jesus answered, 'Neither this man nor his parents sinned,
but that the works of God should be revealed in him. 4 I
must work the works of Him who sent Me while it is day;
the night is coming when no one can work. 5 As long as I
am in the world, I am the light of the world.' 6 When He
had said these things, He spat on the ground and made clay
with the saliva; and He anointed the eyes of the blind man
with the clay. 7 And He said to him, 'Go, wash in the pool of
Siloam' (which is translated, Sent). So he went and washed,
and came back seeing."* (1-7)

The common understanding of this story is that God
caused the man to be born blind so that He could heal him
later. A cursory look at the text seems to justify this view,
but also flies in the face of numerous other texts that
clearly say that Satan is the author of sickness and disease

and that God is the author of healing. Let's see if we can sort out the truth.

One thing to remember when studying the Bible is that the original manuscripts contained only capital letters, no punctuation, and no spaces between words or breaks between sentences. It was up to the reader or translator to sort things out. Let's look at the critical text again.

Looking again at the text as it might have appeared in an original document. I have sketched it out in English, not Greek.

NOWASJESUSPASSEDBYHESAWAMANWHOWASBLINDF
ROMBIRTHANDHISDISCIPLESASKEDHIMSAYINGRABBI
WHOSINNEDTHISMANORHISPARENTSTHATHEWASBOR
NBLINDJESUSANSWEREDNEITHERTHISMANNORHISPAR
ENTSSINNEDBUTTHATTHEWORKSOFGODSHOULDBERE
VEALEDINHIMIMUSTWORKTHEWORKSOFHIMWHOSEN
TMEWHILEITISDAYTHENIGHTISCOMINGWHENNOONEC
ANWORK

It's easy to see how complex was the translation and interpretation of the original document. What if we consider an alternative reading, without changing a word only the punctuation; remembering that the punctuation is not inspired?

"Now as Jesus passed by, He saw a man who was blind from birth. And His disciples asked Him, saying, 'Rabbi, who sinned, this man or his parents, that he was born blind?'"

The question has connection to Jewish beliefs (not necessarily biblical) about persons born blind. They

66

believed that when a person was born blind that it was because of the sins of his parents or that perhaps the child had sinned while in its mother's womb. Thus, the question; "Who sinned..."

Then Jesus answered, *"Neither this man nor his parents sinned"*. Thus at this point, I would ask, did Jesus answer the disciple's question? I believe He did and therefore, we could insert a period at the end of the statement and continue as a new sentence. *"But, (in order) that the works of God should be revealed in him, I must work the works of Him who sent Me while it is day, the night is coming when no one can work."*

This changes the meaning of the statement but not the wording. Instead of saying that God had made him sick so that He could later heal him, Jesus is really saying that the reason why he was sick was neither of the traditional ideas and that the only important thing is to get the kingdom work accomplished. *"So that the works of God might be manifested in this man, it is necessary for me to do the works..."* Immediately Jesus set about doing the works, he spit in the dirt, made it into mud, rubbed the mud in the eyes of the man and sent him to the pool of Siloam to wash. All the healings and miracles of John's gospel are called **signs**. They are not just simple miracles but have specific symbolic meaning. This one is no different. The context reveals the message to the Pharisees, which, in order to stay on our subject we will not try to unravel here, but what is important to our present discussion is, that on purpose, Jesus healed a man who the religious leaders considered born in sin and worthless, for all intents and purposes, to the kingdom of

God. In other words Jesus is saying that this man is important to him and to the kingdom! Praise God!

There are several other texts, that opponents of healing use, to cast doubt on the teaching of healing, (part of the birth-right of all believers). But if anyone is confused by any of these, I believe that if one applies the same principles of Bible interpretation, already taught and applied in this book, one will easily arrive at the truth.

CHAPTER EIGHT

REDEEMED FROM THE CURSE OF THE LAW

READING: Deuteronomy 28; please read the entire chapter before reading the following.

The first fourteen verses of Deuteronomy 28 spell out the blessings of the covenant produced by faithful obedience to Yahweh. It begins—

"Now it shall come to pass, if you diligently obey the voice of the LORD your God, to observe carefully all His commandments which I command you today, that the LORD your God will set you high above all nations of the earth." 2 "And all these blessings shall come upon you and overtake you, because you obey the voice of the LORD your God."

During the time Mary and I were pastoring a church, I taught a Sunday morning message on Deuteronomy 28, called "The Blessing or The Curse." In it, I said that even though believers are under the grace of God, they are still expected to obey the Bible and the Spirit of God. If believers consistently refuse to obey the Word and the spirit of God, the effects of the curse can still manifest in their lives. When I said that, one man who was a church member, jumped up out of his seat muttering something to himself and walked out of the room. I later found out that he had rounded up his children from the Sunday school and taken them home because, as he said, "the pastor was preaching false doctrine." The ironic thing was that, of all the people in the congregation, he represented the clearest example of what I was preaching. He was living under the curse. At the same time, he refused to believe that a Christian could live under a curse. He said it was an Old Testament principle and didn't apply to New Testament believers. However, he was unemployed at the time and had already bankrupted one business that he had purchased with borrowed money. I could fill pages describing the problems in his life and family, but you get the picture. **The grace of God is actually what provides us with the means to live in obedience to God.** It doesn't give us the option of living self-centered lives. The same foul spirits that cause the curse to operate in one's life, causing sickness and poverty to rule, also work to convince the believer that there is no curse operating in their life, thus keeping them in bondage.

Let's go on reading in chapter 28, Deut. from verse fifteen. In verse fifteen, it changes to the curse that comes upon the inhabitants of the land if they live in disobedience to the covenant. In summary, it includes miscarriage, stillborn children, livestock that don't multiply, plagues of devouring insects (locusts), war (especially defeat in war), drought, fear, insanity, confusion blindness, and disease. First, he mentions various diseases and finally, in verse sixty, he says, *"Moreover He will bring back on you all the diseases of Egypt, of which you were afraid, and they shall cling to you."*

Verse sixty one says: *"Also every sickness and every plague, which is not written in the book of this law, will the LORD bring upon you until you are destroyed."*

There are several different beliefs concerning the matter of God's involvement in plagues, war, sickness, and natural disasters. Some believe that God merely allows these things to happen and that when a nation becomes evil, God's protection is diminished and He merely leaves them to their own devices and allows them to self-destruct. Others believe that God is directly involved in causing these things to happen.

The Apostle Paul said, *"Christ has redeemed us from the curse of the law, having become a curse for us (for it is written, 'Cursed is everyone who hangs on a tree'), 14 that the blessing of Abraham might come upon the Gentiles in Christ Jesus, that we might receive the promise of the Spirit through faith."* (Galatians 3:13-14)

Again in verse twenty-nine he says, *"And if you are Christ's, then you are Abraham's seed, and heirs according to the promise."*

All the plagues, diseases and evil things listed in Deuteronomy 28, are part of the curse of the law. And we are redeemed from the curse. That means if we recognize our disobedience and repent, God will lift the curse from off us and our family.

These promises originally given to Abraham are not as some have said, just for the Jews, but are actually good for any committed follower of Christ.
Some have said that since we are delivered by Christ from the curse, then obedience is not an issue and we are under the blessing whether or not we obey. I am convinced that if we decide to walk in disobedience and presume that the blessing will still be upon us, we are sadly mistaken and may pay dearly for our presumption. God weighs the heart and I believe His grace will cover us for sins that are errors of judgment, but if we plan and

71

purpose to sin, presuming that God will cover us in our disobedience, we are mistaken and will face the disciplinary hand of God.

THE DISCIPLINE OF THE LORD

The writer of Hebrews brings light on the subject of the discipline of the Lord.

*"...My son, do not despise the chastening of the Lord, nor be discouraged when you are rebuked by Him; For whom the Lord loves He **chastens**, and **scourges** every son whom He receives."* (12:5,6)

I see a pattern here. The first key word, *chasten,* is translated from the word *piadiao* a verb meaning to correct. The noun for child is *piadian.* The word has to do with correction as to the correction and training of children. A loving father does not come up behind a child who is involved in some sort of mischief and smack him with a stick. The father first instructs and if that doesn't work he scolds the child and explains his mistake. If the mischief continues and the warning is not heeded, the rod of correction is applied. In some countries today, it is against the law to physically discipline children. Governments think that they are smarter than God and apply humanistic principles to family matters and are now reaping the rotten fruit of their ways. Drug addiction, fatherless children, grandparents raising their grandchildren because the parents are drunk or high on drugs, abortion and violence, a whole generation is growing up without morals as the result of this kind of thinking.

I heard a local pastor, from my community ask this question.

"What's going to happen in the next generation when the righteous grandparents, who are raising their grandchildren, have died off and another generation of babies are born to their drug addicted parents and there are no grandparents to raise them?" Think about it! Anyway, enough rabbit trails, let's get back to the subject.

God deals with his children the same way as a righteous father deals with his children. He instructs, if necessary, he scolds, and if disobedience continues, he spanks. God is not abusive and His mercy is everlasting but He reserves the right to spank His disobedient children. He will even spank nations. The end of the passage says, v-8 *"..if you are without chastening, of which all have become partakers, then you are illegitimate and not sons."* The King James version says, *"..then are ye bastards, and not sons."* That ought to get our attention. If we are without discipline, then we are simply children of the devil and not children of God, because God disciplines or chastises His children.

CHAPTER NINE
THE IMPORTANCE OF FORGIVING OTHERS

REFUSING TO FORGIVE OTHERS

After having finished preaching a message on healing in a Central American country, a woman came up, when I gave the invitation to pray for the sick. She told me that she had suffered for ten years with arthritis in her neck, back, knees and other places. As I reached my hand out toward her head the Lord spoke strongly in my spirit, one word, "FORGIVE." This had happened several times before and I knew it meant that there was a need to forgive someone. I asked the lady, "The Bible teaches us that, before we come to God in prayer, we need to be sure we have forgiven all those we might have something against. Is there someone that you might have something against, that you have not forgiven?" She replied, "No, not that I know of."

Again I reached my hand out toward her but it seemed that the Holy Spirit was restraining me again. I said, "Mam, I want you to take a few minutes and pray and ask God to reveal to your heart, whom it might be that you are holding in unforgiveness. Later, I will come back and we will pray. I'm going to go and pray for some other people." After praying for three or four others I returned to the lady and asked if God had indicated anything to her. She replied again, the same way, assuring me that she was not angry with anyone. I wanted to pray for her but the Spirit was restraining me even stronger this time. Without thinking I said, "Look, Mam, you need to find out who it is because I'm not going to pray for you until you forgive." Then I walked away and continued praying for others. The following evening I was preaching again in the same place.

After the message, I offered to pray for the sick. I noticed the woman coming forward again but her face looked different this time. I asked her with a little attitude, "Well, did the Lord finally tell you who it is that you need to forgive?" "No," She replied, "I knew all along." She said, in a voice loud enough for the crowd to hear. Some started laughing. Continuing, she said, "My husband abandoned me twenty years ago and I swore I would never forgive him, but when I realized that you weren't going to pray for me unless I forgave him, I decided to do it and I'm ready for my healing."

I led this dear sister in a short prayer of repentance and forgiveness and then prayed for her to be healed. The arthritis disappeared immediately and she raised her hands up and praised God saying, that she was pain free for the first time in years.

I have seen scores of people healed in similar manners. It seems that about 75% of all cases of arthritis have roots in bitterness and unforgiveness. Many other infirmities also are related to unforgiveness. The New Testament is clear in its mandate to forgive others if we want to be forgiven by God.

WHAT DOES IT MEAN TO FORGIVE?
To forgive means to drop it, put it away, forget it and go on as if nothing happened. I have had a person, who had left an abusive situation, say to me, "If I forgive him, then I will have to allow him to come back into the house and continued to abuse me and my children." No, forgiveness does not mean that you have to expose yourself to that

kind of thing. It simply means to detach yourself from the situation in such a way that you can move forward with your life and not allow the perpetrator to continue to influence your life from afar.

Another friend asked, "Is it always necessary to go to the person and forgive them in person or can I do it in prayer between myself and God alone?" The answer is, that one needs to handle these things in prayer and by the revelation of the Spirit. I would say that unless the Holy Spirit directs you to bring up the issue, you can deal with it with the Lord alone. When it comes to offences you have committed against others it is usually a good idea to go and ask the person for forgiveness directly but even in this, there are occasions where it is not a good idea. I know of a case where a man became a believer and was having an affair with his friend's wife. He then went and asked forgiveness of his friend which, subsequently, ruined his relationship with his friend and worse, the marriage ended up in divorce.

WHY SHOULD WE FORGIVE OTHERS?
WE ARE CALLED TO MANIFEST THE LOVE NATURE OF CHRIST

Unforgiveness is a manifestation of hatred. Hatred is the opposite of love. Love is the nature of God. Hatred is the nature of Satan. Therefore, if you live in hatred (unforgiveness) you are manifesting the character and nature of Satan. We are called as believers to manifest the character and nature of Christ in this present evil age.

IT PROVIDES PERSONAL BENEFIT

Obedience to God's commands always produce future benefits. As N.T. Wright states, "The rules are to be understood, not as arbitrary laws thought up by a distant God to stop us from having fun (or to set up some ethical hoops to jump through as a kind of moral examination), but as the signposts to a way of life in which heaven and earth overlap, in which God's future breaks into the present, in which we discover what genuine humanness looks and feels like in practice."[10]

The concept of forgiving others is difficult and even painful for many to think about. I have often said, **"Growing up in Christ begins with doing things we don't want to do when we don't want to do them."** During periods of outpourings of the Holy Spirit I have seen Him overpower people, flattening them on the floor for hours, sometimes even giving them visions, putting them in trances, sometimes for hours or even days. We might wish for these experiences to be the key to instant spiritual maturity but no matter what experiences we have, we always end up coming out of them and after that, we have to continue to deal with the flesh much the same as before.

When you first start out on this path you will encounter a serious battle with the flesh. Your flesh will not want to forgive, it will rebel and come up with a dozen reasons why you shouldn't forgive. You need to just tell your flesh to shut up! and let your spirit overrule your flesh and win the victory. After continually dealing with the flesh and forgiving again and again, your flesh and carnal mind will

---

[10] Wright, N.T. Simply Christian; 2006; Pg.229

begin to come into line and give you less flack about it. There are, however, great benefits to obeying Jesus' command to forgive.

JESUS COMMANDED US TO FORGIVE

Mark 11:25,26; *"And whenever you stand praying, if you have anything against anyone, forgive him, that your Father in heaven may also forgive you your trespasses. 26 But if you do not forgive, neither will your Father in heaven forgive your trespasses."*

This text reveals several things to us. First, that we must forgive no matter what the offense is, *"..anything against anyone."* Secondly, he says, "and when you stand praying." We can't wait around for our feelings to agree with our actions; we must forgive while we are still praying. And third, that our extending forgiveness to others is directly connected to our being continually forgiven by God.

Forgiving is an act of faith, not based on feelings or emotions.
Some have said, that to forgive someone, when I have not yet been delivered from all negative emotions, is not genuine, nor honest. Acts of faith are not governed or dependent upon our feelings and emotions. Obeying God is never dishonest.

Jesus calls us to forgive anyone who has wronged us, even those who continue to wrong us in the present and have not asked us to forgive them. Some have tried to make a case for being able to wait until the perpetrator has come asking forgiveness of us. You may be waiting a long time and meanwhile, the venom of unforgiveness, will be eating away at your body and soul. Have you ever noticed how much more difficult it is to enter into the presence of the Lord when you are angry? That fact alone should convince us that to forgive is a valuable ability, unless you enjoy the frustration of desiring to come into the presence of God and finding it nearly impossible.

FORGIVENESS RELEASES PERSONAL FREEDOM

A person who dwells in bitterness, anger, resentment, defensiveness secludes himself behind walls of self-protection. We convince ourselves that these walls are necessary to protect us but we fail to realize that they actually imprison us behind the walls that we have build inhibiting our freedom. Forgiving others sets us free from the prison of self and neutralized numerous poisonous emotions that tend to control us. I remember a little known Bible teacher saying, "Refusing to forgive is like drinking poison and hoping that your enemy dies from it."

UNFORGIVENESS RELEASES THE POWERS OF DARKNESS TO TORMENT US

Matthew 18:21-35; "Then Peter came to Him and said, 'Lord, how often shall my brother sin against me, and I forgive him? Up to seven times?' 22 Jesus said to him, 'I do not say to you, up to seven times, but up to seventy times seven. 23 Therefore the kingdom of heaven is like a certain king who wanted to settle accounts with his servants. 24 And when he had begun to settle accounts, one was brought to him who owed him ten thousand talents. 25 But as he was not able to pay, his master commanded that he be sold, with his wife and children and all that he had, and that payment be made. 26 'The servant therefore fell down before him, saying, 'Master, have patience with me, and I will pay you all.' 27 Then the master of that servant was moved with compassion, released him, and forgave him the debt. But that servant went out and found one of his fellow servants who owed him a hundred denarii; and he laid hands on him and took him by the throat, saying, 'Pay me what you owe!' 29 So his fellow servant fell down at his feet and begged him, saying, 'Have patience with me, and I will pay you all.' 30 And he would not, but went and threw him into prison till he should pay the debt. 31 So when his fellow servants saw what had been done, they were very grieved, and came and told their master all that had been done. 32 "Then his master, after he had called him, said to him, 'You wicked servant! I forgave you all that debt because you begged me. 33 'Should you not also have had compassion on your fellow servant, just as I had pity on you?' 34 "And his master was angry, and delivered him to the **torturers** until he should pay all that was due to him. 35 "So My heavenly Father also will do to you if each of you, from his heart, does not forgive his brother his trespasses."

Remember, talents in the Bible are not talents, like the ability to play a musical instrument. A talent is a unit of solid measure by weight.,usually a bar of gold or silver. When used as a measure of money, it refers to a **talent-weight of gold or of silver**. Some authorities state that the talent typically weighed about 33 kg (75 lb). The international price of gold is presently about $800 per troy ounce, i.e. about $25 per gram. At this price, a talent (33 kg) would be worth about $825,000. Therefore the man in question owed his master $8 billion USD, obviously a totally unpayable amount since he was not the owner of a Fortune 500 company but a slave! The master grants forgiveness of the unpardonable debt and soon, thereafter, the same man finds a fellow slave who owes him a hundred denarii. A denarii was one of the smallest silver coins weighing 3 grams at that time, therefore this amount (300 grams) didn't add up to even a pound of silver. (453g.= 1lb.)

This parable puts foreword a serious warning to those who would refuse to forgive. The man was delivered to the torturers. This must be a reference to the powers of darkness, the demons, who are released to attack them.

All committed followers of Jesus Christ have all been released from the unpardonable debt because of God's covenant mercy. We then, are expected to act like God and forgive others. The man who refused to forgive his fellow servant was turned over to the tormentors. Jesus' explanation of the parable is unmistakable.

"So My heavenly Father also will do to you if each of you, from his heart, does not forgive his brother his trespasses."

What does this look like? What happens to one who is turned over to the tormentors?

First: the unforgiving person tends to become like the one he has refused to forgive.

We see this over and over again. The son of the alcoholic who emphatically states, "I will never be like my dad, I will never drink." And then soon becomes an alcoholic himself. Why? The refusal to forgive makes the unforgiver a prisoner of the unforgiven.

Second: Maintaining unforgiveness consumes large portions of the thought life of the unforgiver. Every minute I spend thinking about a person that I hold something against is a minute of my life controlled by that person. The more time I spend thinking about this offense, the more it will seem to grow in my imagination and seem worse in my thinking, and thus, tormenting me.

Third: Unforgiveness can be the source of numerous physical ailments. Thus physical torment occurs.

Forth: Unforgiveness will cause one to be grouchy and hard to live with, thus it will poison relationships with the people we love as well.

Torment is the operative word in this parable. No one really desires to be tormented but when we refuse to forgive we automatically release torment into our lives.

THE CORE OF THE GOSPEL
If someone were to ask you, "What verse of scripture presents the pivotal issue of the gospel?" How would you answer? Most Christians I have asked that question, have answered with John 3:16; *"For God so loved the world..."*
But if you were able to ask one of the first century church fathers like Justin Martyr who sat at the feet of John, The Apostle or Clement of Rome, who was a disciple of Paul, they would have said something entirely different. Both of them and many others believed that the core issue of the gospel was summed up in Matthew 5:44; *"But I say to you, love your enemies, bless those who curse you, do good to those who hate you, and pray for those who spitefully use you and persecute you ..."*

All of the early church fathers believed that we come to Christ, just as we are but that remaining unchanged is not an option. None of them would have displayed on their donkey cart the popular bumper sticker that said, "Christians aren't perfect, just forgiven." For them the core issue of being a Christian was not "whether or not you are going to heaven when you die" as popular modern day evangelical theology would express it. They believed that faith in Jesus Christ, without a corresponding lifestyle change, was simply dead, and not really faith at all.

FORGIVING AND FORGETING
EPH 4:32 *And be kind to one another, tenderhearted, forgiving one another, just as God in Christ also forgave you.*

The operative phrase here is "just as" meaning that we must forgive *in the same way* as God forgives us. So how does God forgive us?

"I, even I, am He who blots out your transgressions for My own sake; and I will not remember your sins."
(Isaiah 43:25)

"He will again have compassion on us, and will subdue our iniquities. You will cast all our sins into the depths of the sea." (Micah 7:19)

"For I will be merciful to their unrighteousness, and their sins and their lawless deeds I will remember no more."
(Hebrews 8:12; 10:17)

These statements of how the Lord forgives and expects us to forgive others often make people nervous on two different fronts. First, we think, "How can I do that? I can't just make myself forget." It's true that, in myself, I have no strength to actually forget the evil that others have done to me. But Jesus is all powerful and completely capable of changing a mind that is fully submitted to him. Some Christians waste their lives away stewing about past hurts that they can do nothing about, marinating in bitterness and anger. Not only is this anger a waste of time, it rots out their intestines, knots up their joints with arthritis, and keeps them awake at night.

The second issue we have with this is that it makes us feel vulnerable. We think that if we really forgive, we will immediately be obliged to allow this person back into our lives and continue the cycle of abuse. This is not the case, forgiving is one thing, restored relationships are another. You can forgive an evil person but only by the clear leading of the Holy Spirit are you required to restore relationship with the person.

Often a person's anger toward others is actually anger against God, but they are too religious to admit, even to themselves, that they are angry at God for allowing evil things to happen to them. Some need to come to terms with this and forgive God.

EVIL TRANSFORMED INTO GOOD
Some, who recognize that they need to forgive, but have difficulty in doing so, attempt to transform the evil that has been done to them into good. Well, maybe not exactly good, but "not so evil." This is how it goes: Fred's father

was a raging alcoholic and came home drunk and beat up his wife and kids. Bill, his son (not their real names), in order to forgive says to himself, "Well, my grandfather was an alcoholic as well, he beat my father and therefore my father was psychologically damaged and couldn't help it. Then we transform alcoholism from a sin to a disease, further distancing the perpetrator from his crimes. We think that by this process we are forgiving, but actually we are just "putting lipstick on the pig" and not forgiving, transforming evil into good. We need to recognize sin as sin, crime as crime, abuse as abuse. We need to face it head on and call it what it is—evil. Then we need to forgive the evil that was perpetrated against us, no matter how evil the act was.

HOW DO WE FORGIVE?
If, during the reading of this chapter, you have thought of people that have done you wrong and you have not forgiven them or you have tried to forgive them but every time you think of them your mind rehearses the scenario of evil, then I want you to pray a prayer with me for forgiveness and release.

Pray this with me:
Heavenly father, I recognize that one of your commands is to forgive. I want to obey you in this and extend the forgiveness that you extended to me from the cross for my sins. Therefore I forgive _____ for what they did to me (state the evil done in detail) I release _____ from all desire that I have held onto that (s)he should be punished for their sins.
I ask you to bless _____ and draw him/her closer to you.

I ask you Father to forgive me for my failure to forgive. I ask you to release me from the grasp of the tormentors and to help me forget what was done to me. Thank you for hearing my prayer.

Repeat this prayer for each person that you need to forgive.

Now every time you think of that person or see them, pray briefly for blessing on their life.

In conclusion: Recognize that forgiving others is of extreme importance concerning your health and well-being, both spiritual, mental and physical. Don't wait, do it now!

CHAPTER TEN

THE TEMPLE OF GOD

REV 3:12 *"He who overcomes, I will make him a pillar in the temple of My God, and he shall go out no more. And I will write on him the name of My God and the name of the city of My God, the New Jerusalem, which comes down out of heaven from My God. And I will write on him My new name."*

N.T. Wright taught that there were four things that comprised the Jewish expectation of the fulfillment of the kingdom.

One: The Torah (the word of God) Two: the land. Three: the temple and Four: Jewish ethnic identity.
Wright concluded that all these things are fulfilled in Messiah, Jesus. The Jews were not satisfied, however, with Herod's Temple, which was a poor replica of the Temple of Solomon. They would not have even been satisfied with an exact duplication of Solomon's Temple as majestic and beautiful as it was unless it was accompanied by the outpouring of the "shekkinah" (the manifest visible presence of Yahweh) and the fire of God coming down and consuming the sacrifices.

Jesus is the true fulfillment of the above. Jesus is the living word, the Logos of God. He is the promised land, true life is only lived in him. He is the true Temple, the dwelling place of the Holy Spirit. Finally, he is the true Jew
Jesus, speaking of Himself said:

"'Destroy this temple, and in three days I will raise it up.' 20 Then the Jews said, 'It has taken forty-six years to build this temple, and will You raise it up in three days?' 21 But He was speaking of the temple of His body." (JOH 2:19-21)

This he spoke of his own resurrection from the dead but the apostle Paul spoke of a more extended meaning of "his body" referring to the church.

"Do you not know that you are the temple of God and that the Spirit of God dwells in you?"

(1CO 3:16)

I believe that if we are able to have a clear revelation of who we are in Christ and that, we are indeed, the dwelling place of God himself (and even more than that is true) we would not only think differently but we would live differently. Many believers are comfortable with the concept of the Holy Spirit dwelling in our spirit but the idea of the Spirit making his dwelling place in our mortal bodies makes them a bit nervous. Even though many believers probably don't even know what dualism is, we are still victims of that kind of mentality. Dualism is the idea that all spirit is good and that the material world is entirely evil and corrupted. This idea crept into Christianity from Greek philosophy. The concept has nothing to do with true biblical Christianity. *"Or do you not know that your body is the temple of the Holy Spirit who is in you,"* (2Cor. 6:19)

Remember that in the Creation, God created the body first from the basic elements that He had already made. Then He blew into the man's nose His own breath, the breath of life, and man became a living being. (Gen 2:7) There is no indication in any of the dialogue about creation that one part was better than another part. Seven times in the first chapter of Genesis God spoke about the creation and said it was **good**, the last one of which He said it was "very good." In fact, He was so pleased with what he created that he took a day off just to contemplate what He had done. The pinnacle of the created order and culmination of all God's work was the creation of man. He never said, "Well, I made his spirit good but will just have to put up with this bad old body." No, it was all good, it was all excellent, a perfect creation.

So ask yourself this question, "if my body is the temple of the Holy Spirit why would the Holy Spirit want to share His temple with what we've already determined to be Satanic products like sickness and disease?" The answer is obvious, there is no place in Christ's body for sickness anymore than there is a place for demons. When a person receives Christ as his Savior and Lord, if there are demons inhabiting that vessel, then the war begins between the Spirit of God, who wants to fully inhabit that vessel and the demons that He sets about to kick out. I've never found a Christian yet who believed it was God's will for a Christian to have demons.

But I found many Christians who believe that it's God's will for Christians to be sick. I've even read books by Christians who prayed for sickness to come on them. Isn't that interesting, we believe that Satanic agents called demons are not supposed to dwell in a Christian but we will accept that Satanic products or things caused by demons could not only dwell there but that it might be the will of God that they dwell there. This is nonsense! God wants us free of demons and free of disease. I like to confess out loud, "My body is the temple of the Holy

Spirit! Sickness, disease and demons are all off limits in my body and have no authority in me, more over, any member of my family or the family of God that He has put in my care."

CHAPTER ELEVEN

FAITH and HEALING

There is a clear connection in both the new and the Old Testament between healing and faith. Remember the passage in Mark chapter 5 that we talked about earlier concerning the woman with the issue of blood? After she was healed Jesus spoke the following words to her. *"Daughter, your faith has made you well. Go in peace, and be healed of your affliction."* (v-34)

Again in Matthew 9:29 Jesus ministered to two blind men and touching their eyes he said, *"According to your faith let it be to you."*

In many instances throughout the gospel record Jesus commented on the faith of different people. He also rebuked his disciples for not having faith or having "little faith." Many people are very confused about faith and what it really is and isn't. Most Christians think that faith and trust are virtually synonymous but we will see that they are actually quite different. The whole issue is not as complicated as some people would like to make it. The noun, *faith*, and the verb, *believe*, come from the same root word in the old and the New Testament.

FAITH: WHAT IS IT?

The writer of Hebrews said in chapter 11:1; *"Now faith is the substance of things hoped for, the evidence of things not seen."*

The words substance, used here is a very powerful word. The Greek word is *hupostasis*. In Hebrews, it seems to take on the concept of reality itself, thus the King James rendering *substance*. Some translations have followed Luther's unfortunate choice of *confidence*.

Like the New International Version which says, "Faith is being sure.."

Luther's influence caused the understanding of faith to take on the idea of "personal subjective[11] conviction"[12] disregarding the fact that the Hebrew and Greek understanding of the word, including virtually all of the church fathers assumed the understanding of objective[13] demonstration and proof, i.e. substance. This concept is underscored by the use of the word in chapter 1 verse 3 where it says regarding Jesus, " *who being the brightness of His glory and the express image of His person,*" here *hupostasis* is translated *person.* W.E. Vine states, "it speaks of the **divine essence** of God existent and expressed in the revelation of His Son."

GEN 12:1-4; *Now the LORD had said to Abram: "Get out of your country, from your kindred and from your father's house, to a land that I will show you. 2 I will make you a great nation; I will bless you and make your name great; and you shall be a blessing. 3 I will bless those who bless you, and I will curse him who curses you; and in you all the families of the earth shall be blessed." 4 So Abram departed as the LORD had spoken to him, and Lot went*

---

[11] Subjective: taking place within the mind and modified by individual bias; "a subjective judgment"
[12] For a more complete understanding see Kittel's Theological Dictionary of The New Testament; VIII, p 572-589
[13] Objective: undistorted by emotion or personal bias; based on observable phenomena; "an objective appraisal"; "objective evidence"

with him. And Abram was seventy-five years old when he departed from Haran.

The biblical concept of faith is so closely interwoven with obedience that some Old Testament commentators have called it obedience/faith. Note that God spoke to Abraham and gave him a threefold command; *"Get out of your country, from your kindred and from your father's house, to a land that I will show you."* In other words leave your nation, your town and your family; don't look back, I will show you the place where you're going as you move forward. For Abraham this must have been a totally frightening and counterculture event.

People in those days did not have government, law and police to protect them. They depended on family and extended relationships outside the family unit for protection from people, or nations who might decide to harm them. Therefore, to take off on your own with only your immediate family was a dangerous undertaking. The territory was inhabited by bandits, one could be robbed, enslaved or worse. This is the beginning of faith, accepting the word of another as truth and totally reliable. Expecting that a word spoken will come to pass as it was said, or if the word was spoken as already a fact, accepting that word as fact even though it speaks of an unseen reality, is faith! When we accept God's word as fact, His power comes to bear on the situation causing the word to become flesh so to speak, 'substance.'

Many people have a serious misunderstanding of how faith operates in the life of the believer. They are critical of those who believe that faith will cause things to change. They make up slogans such as, "name it and claim it" or "super faith." They say, "those people think that they can order God around and just tell God what to do." I admit that there are people out there who have attempted to use faith in this way and some have even taught it that way, but they are few in number and don't last very long. The biblical understanding of faith is not to tell God what to do but to find out what God wants to do and get in agreement with Him. To understand what He has already said as fact and to believe that it will actually happen in your life.

That's precisely what happened with Abraham. I love using Abraham as an example of faith for two reasons. First, Abraham wasn't a preacher, an apostle or a prophet but he was a cattleman who lived in a tent in the desert. God spoke to him and called him out and his life was never the same after that. The other thing I like about Abraham is that he was much like you and me, that he made mistakes, he didn't do it all perfectly. Many preachers, when they talk about Abraham make him out to be some kind of magic man that perfectly obeyed God at every turn but as we go through the narrative we see that Abraham wasn't always perfect. He made mistakes and God worked things out anyway. Now, I'm not saying that we should make mistakes, nor am I making excuses for disobedience but Abraham's heart was after God and despite his mistakes, God blessed him. He received a sevenfold promise and a threefold command. If he had not believed that God would fulfill his sevenfold promise there would be no reason for him to obey the threefold command. He had no previous history with God and no testimony of God's deeds from time past. Yahweh just appeared to him out of nowhere and talked to him this way.

Joshua 24:2,3; tells us that Abraham and his fathers, formerly worshiped idols when they lived in Mesopotamia. Rabbinic tradition has it that Abraham was an idol maker by trade; they had totally departed from the faith that his ancestor Noah had in Yahweh. He didn't know Yahweh and had no reason for confidence in him.

Note that when Yahweh called Abraham he said, *".. My covenant is with you, and you shall be a father of many nations." At a time when both Abraham and his wife Sarah were past childbearing years God says that Abraham will be a father of many nations. In the next sentence he continues, "No longer shall your name be called Abram, but your name shall be Abraham; for I have made you a father of many nations.* (GEN 17:4,5)

God ordains the future, calling it into existence and immediately calls it done, and states it as if it had already come to pass. In Abraham's time dimension it took over four hundred years for God's decree to become a visible reality. For Yahweh it was done as soon as he said it. Why? Paul answers this in part, talking about Abraham in Romans 4:17-21;

"..as it is written, 'I have made you a father of many nations' in the presence of Him whom he believed, even God, who gives life to the dead and calls those things which do not exist as though they did; 18 who, contrary to hope, in hope believed, so that he became the father of many nations, according to what was spoken, "So shall your descendants be." 19 And not being weak in faith, he did not consider his own body, already dead (since he was about a hundred years old), and the deadness of Sarah's womb. 20 He did not waver at the promise of God through unbelief,

95

but was strengthened in faith, giving glory to God, 21 and being fully convinced that what He had promised He was also able to perform."

Abraham, after much hesitation decided to agree with God and go along with His program. He refused to consider the physical, visible circumstances i.e. that he was nearly a hundred years old and his wife nearly ninety. Verse 20 says that, *"He did not waver at the promise of God.."* Abraham refused to wobble back and forth between believing and disbelieving what God had said. The word waver means to "double-judge" The King James Version says "stagger" You are looking at two different sets of evidence, on the one hand the testimony of the natural circumstances saying, "you are too old, it's too late, it's not going to happen" and the testimony of God that looks from the heavenly time into earthly time and says, *"I have made you the father of many nations."* Abraham finally decided to fix his eyes on God's promise and believe that, in the face of all contradictory evidence, once he agreed with God, it was locked in.

This problem with "staggering" is what causes most of our problems with faith. God gives His promise but we want the circumstances to line up with God's promise before we actually believe. For the most part we are just hoping that things come out all right. We think God is good so we trust that somehow He will make it right. None of that is really faith.

Let's go back to Hebrews 11 and look at a couple of the examples given there. First Noah:
Verse 7 *"By faith Noah, being divinely warned of things not yet seen, moved with godly fear, prepared an ark for*

the saving of his household, by which he condemned the world and became heir of the righteousness which is according to faith."

Notice what it says here, *"Noah being divinely warned of things not yet seen..."* being divinely warned means that he received the word of God; God's warning of the flood that was coming on the earth. Thus he moved in obedience to the divine command and through his obedience saved his whole household, not to mention the animals.

In the following verse we find another statement about Abraham,
"By faith Abraham obeyed when he was called to go out to the place which he would afterward receive as an inheritance. And he went out, not knowing where he was going." We find the same sequence of events, Abraham was called and he obeyed. In order to obey, Abraham had to be absolutely convinced of two factors concerning the God who spoke, first, that He was capable of fulfilling His word (power) and secondly, that He wasn't a liar and actually desired to fulfill His word. (*truthfulness*)

We could go on, and speak of Sarah, Moses, Gideon, Barak, Samson, Jephthah, and also of David, Samuel and the prophets; all of them moved by faith doing the things that they accomplished in the same manner, but I think we've made our point.

NEW TESTAMENT FAITH
Let's take a look in an interesting example from the New Testament. The New Testament is filled with stories of great exploits of faith and the things that many different

men and women of God accomplished. Read the following narrative of Peter's life from the book of Acts and then we'll comment on it:

12:1 "Now about that time Herod the king stretched out his hand to harass some from the church. 2 Then he killed James the brother of John with the sword. 3 And because he saw that it pleased the Jews, he proceeded further to seize Peter also. Now it was during the Days of Unleavened Bread. 4 So when he had apprehended him, he put him in prison, and delivered him to four squads of soldiers to keep him, intending to bring him before the people after Passover.

5 Peter was therefore kept in prison, but constant prayer was offered to God for him by the church. 6 And when Herod was about to bring him out, that night Peter was sleeping, bound with two chains between two soldiers; and the guards before the door were keeping the prison. 7 Now behold, an angel of the Lord stood by him, and a light shone in the prison; and he struck Peter on the side and raised him up, saying, 'Arise quickly!' And his chains fell off his hands. 8 Then the angel said to him, 'Gird yourself and tie on your sandals'; and so he did. And he said to him, 'Put on your garment and follow me.' 9 So he went out and followed him, and did not know that what was done by the angel was real, but thought he was seeing a vision. 10 When they were past the first and the second guard posts, they came to the iron gate that leads to the city, which opened to them of its own accord; and they went out and went down one street, and immediately the angel departed from him. 11 And when Peter had come to himself, he said, 'Now I know for certain that the Lord has sent His angel, and has delivered me from the hand of Herod and from all the expectation of the Jewish people.'

12 So, when he had considered this, he came to the house of Mary, the mother of John whose surname was Mark, where many were gathered together praying. 13 And as Peter knocked at the door of the gate, a girl named Rhoda came to answer. 14 When she recognized Peter's voice, because of her gladness she did not open the gate, but ran in and announced that Peter stood before the gate. 15 But they said to her, "You are beside yourself!" Yet she kept insisting that it was so. So they said, "It is his angel. 16 Now Peter continued knocking; and when they opened the door and saw him, they were astonished."

What happened with Peter in the story is easy to miss. Here, James is already killed by Herod, (that's James the apostle, not James the Lord's brother). When Herod sees that the people like it, he arrests Peter and locks him up in prison and intends to kill him soon after the Passover. The night before Peter is to be executed, he is chained between two soldiers and there are two other soldiers nearby, but Peter is asleep laying on the dirty block floor, chained between soldiers. What would you be doing, if you are in that position? Would you be sleeping? I don't think I would be. I don't know what method of execution Herod had planned, but they were never nice. There was no such thing as lethal injection. Without a doubt Herod had some plan that he would use to make an example of Peter. If I was Peter I probably would've been up trying to think of all the sins I had ever committed to confess them to God before morning. But Peter was sleeping. What was it that caused him to be so filled with peace that he could get a good night sleep when they had told them he would be executed the following day? First of all, the man who had formerly denied Christ had come to terms with his own fallibility and had dispossessed himself of the ownership of his own life. He placed his life absolutely in the hands of Jesus but there is something else going on here. Peter may have received promises from Jesus concerning his life and ministry but he definitely had received promises concerning his death concerning his death. When Peter was restored back to full relationship and ministry (John 21) Jesus gave him the following word in verse eighteen:

"Most assuredly, I say to you, when you were younger, you girded yourself and walked where you wished; but when you are old, you will stretch out your hands, and another will gird you and carry you where you do not wish." 19 This He spoke, signifying by what death he would glorify God."

This remark of Jesus, in our language seems somewhat cryptic and we are not sure exactly what they meant in the language that Jesus spoke. Maybe even Peter didn't fully understand the words at the time that Jesus gave them but the apostle John later wrote that those words indicated the type of death that Peter would suffer. We know from the writings of Clement of Rome (C. A.D. 96) that Peter was martyred. We find out later from Tertullian (C. AD 212) that Peter was actually crucified. So Peter is lying between two guards chained. In his mind I'm sure he believed the word was being fulfilled that Jesus had given him,
"another will bind you and carry you where you do not wish," yet he is in such peace that he is able to lay down and go to sleep. He slept so sound that the angel had to kick him in the ribs to wake him up.

There is faith for living, there is faith for being delivered from bad situations, there is faith for healing but there is also faith for dying, dying to self, dying to all our self-made plans, our dreams and aspirations. That faith allows one to live in peace, even when the natural outlook of things indicates that you won't be around to see another day. There's no way to know exactly what was going through Peter's mind that day. Maybe Jesus told him he was going to be delivered, maybe he didn't. Peter was so shocked when the angel came and delivered him that he thought it was a dream. The first thing he did after he got out of jail was to head straight over to the prayer meeting. The next day he went straight to the Temple to preach the word of God. The men who had caused him to be put in jail the first time must have been close by. We want everything God tells us to do to make sense. What Peter did, made no sense at all from a natural perspective but to God, who knows the end from the beginning, it made perfect sense. Before we endeavor to set out on this journey of a life of faith we must first settle the issue of ownership. Who do we belong to, God or ourselves?

So then we see, that faith must be developed by diligently meditating in God's word. But what really happens when we meditate in God's word? We get to know God better, as Paul prayed for the Ephesians church, that they "..might increase in the knowledge of God." When we know God in a deep and profound way, faith becomes a natural outworking of that knowledge. We begin to understand God's character, his desires, His plan for our lives as well as His power. It becomes increasingly easy to put absolute confidence in what He has said about us in His word. So, faith is being totally convinced that what

God has said, is already accomplished even when it doesn't look like it. When we get into agreement with God and believe the same thing that He believes, we say the same thing that He is saying, then faith becomes "substance" and the result is forthcoming.

Don't get upset if you try to put some of these things to work in your life and they don't work perfectly at first. Living by faith is a learning process and it doesn't come instantly.

CHAPTER TWELVE

THE SACRAMENTS AND HEALING

In the early 1980's I ministered in Honduras with some precious brothers who had formerly been Quakers. While they have great understanding of scripture in many areas, their founder, George Fox whom I quoted in Chapter One, believed that the sacraments of baptism and the Lord's Supper were symbols that spoke of a greater spiritual reality and did not really need to be physically practiced in the present day. I spoke about it with the primary leader who later asked me to teach on the Lord's Supper and then serve it to his leadership core. After a short biblical exposition on the subject, we ate together from the Lord's Table. The power of the Holy Spirit fell in a dramatic way and it seemed that there wasn't a dry eye in the room. Most of them fell to their knees and were silent before the Lord for several minutes.

Personally I gained a new understanding of the majesty of what I like to refer to as **the covenant meal**. My charismatic Quaker friends also gained a powerful insight and soon, the communion became a regular part of their gatherings.

One thing I failed to realize at that time was the underlying reason for Fox's hesitance to embrace the covenant meal. This, I believe, was *dualism*, a belief that crept into the church from the influence of Greek philosophy, around the third century and has never really gone away and has done damage to the Church ever sense. Dualism is basically the belief that matter is evil and spirit is good. This belief has led to such false beliefs as sex is a necessary evil, we need sex to procreate but we should only have sex for that purpose and not for enjoyment. This belief is still held in the Roman Catholic Church and among some Pentecostals. These beliefs have reduced the sacraments to rather empty symbols. We are not sure what exactly they mean and what they are suppose to accomplish in our lives.

We must remember that God created the physical world and everything in it. Over and over He said it was **good**. I believe He was so excited about what He had created, that He took a day off in order to contemplate His own handiwork.

Others approach the sacraments as ways that we can earn points with God. We please Him by being obedient in these things and later we get some sort of blessing in this world or, at least, in the world to come. This of course, doesn't work and actually is counter- productive to the real benefits.

Dualism has also caused many to view physical healing as an almost irrelevant side issue to the gospel. Jesus didn't seem to view it that way.

To understand the **sacraments** we must go back to the Exodus and join with our close cousins, the Jewish people, at the time of their escape from bondage in Egypt. They had spent over 400 years in Egypt, first as welcome guests because of Joseph. Then, when Pharaoh died and another took his place, the present pharaoh became fearful as the Hebrew guests were multiplying and becoming wealthy and powerful. He confiscated their wealth and forced them into servitude. Finally, God raised up Moses as a deliverer and after training him for forty years in the desert, he was sent by God to demand the freedom of his people. After releasing a dozen curses on the Egyptians, finally God gave Moses specific instructions for killing the Passover lamb, sprinkling his blood on the door posts, eating the whole lamb and causing them to be protected from wrath of the final curse against the firstborn of Egypt. Yahweh said, *"When I see the blood I will pass over you."* The Israelites were protected and shortly after that delivered from bondage. Not only that, but first they collected up the silver and gold of Egypt and on the Passover night, every sick, lame, crippled, blind or otherwise weakened, Israelite was healed and made strong for a long walk in the desert. There were no wheelchairs, stretchers or other conveyances for any elderly or infirm people because the whole nation was made strong and fit for the journey.

"He brought them forth also with silver and gold: and there was not one feeble person among their tribes. Egypt was glad when they departed: for the fear of them fell upon them." (Psalms 105:37,38)

At the last Passover that Jesus shared with his disciples, *"..as they were eating, Jesus took bread, blessed it and broke it, and gave it to the disciples and said, 'Take, eat; this is my body.' Then He took the cup, and gave thanks, and gave it to them, saying, 'Drink from it, all of you. For this is my blood of the new covenant, which is shed for many for the remission of sins.'"* (Mat. 26:26-28) (Mark 14:22-27; Luke 22:14-23; John 13:18)

The Apostle Paul echo's the statement of Jesus, saying, *"...For indeed Christ, our Passover, was sacrificed for us."* (1Cor. 5:7)

Jesus connected himself symbolically with the Passover supper in which every Hebrew was instantly healed of all his infirmities at once. As Bible believing Christians we need to develop our understanding of what a **blood covenant** is and how God includes us in the covenant He made with us, sealed in the **blood of his son, Jesus**. When we, as a group of believers, sit at the Lord's Table and partake of the bread and the wine in the small fellowship that I am a part of, we eat from one common loaf and drink from one common cup. We do this to remind ourselves that we are one body in Christ and that we partake of one blood. We don't use little bread wafers and a little plastic individual servings of wine because we recognize that this covenant meal is not a private individualized affair. It is a corporate meal that we take together. We recognize our oneness in Christ not just within the local congregation but with the entire body of Christ worldwide.

WHAT ABOUT TRANSUBSTANTIATION?
The Roman Catholic Church doctrine states that the bread and wine of the communion meal literally and physically are transformed into the body and blood of the Lord Jesus as soon as an authorized representative of the Church blesses it in the prescribed manner. They use 1Cor. 11:23-26 to prove this teaching.

"For I received from the Lord that which I also delivered to you: that the Lord Jesus on the same night in which He

106

was betrayed took bread; and when He had given thanks, He broke it and said, *"Take, eat; **this is My body** which is broken for you; do this in remembrance of Me. In the same manner He also took the cup after supper, saying, "This **cup is the new covenant in my blood.** This do, as often as you drink it, in remembrance of me. For as often as you eat this bread and drink this cup, you proclaim the Lord's death till He comes."*

On the other side of the ledger, most evangelical Christians view the Covenant meal as a mere symbol that for some reason or other, the Lord has instructed us to partake of, but little or no faith is applied to the eating toward receiving some benefit and usually it is an empty ritual that we go through the motions of taking once a month or so. The truth lies somewhere between these two diverse opinions. Certainly, when the elements are taken and digested they become part of the body of a believer and thus since that believer is part of the body of Christ, the elements become part of Christ's body.

I believe that the covenant meal is not so much a miracle of transformed substance as a miracle of time. When we sit down together and break bread we enter into the eternal realm. We enter into God's time and space dimension. We sit by faith with the Israelites at the first Passover, with Abraham as he sat with Christ and ate with him and two angels (Gen 18) with Ruth (a type of the Church) , when Boaz (a type of Christ) invited her, even though she was a Moabites, to share in a meal with him and later she became his wife (Ruth 2:14); with the disciples of Jesus at the last Passover Seder, and at the marriage supper of the Lamb with every believer past, present and future. You might ask, "How can this be so?"

107

We understand that every believer is "in Christ" and when a believer dies he is still in Christ. Therefore, we are together in Christ. A person who is not yet born again, yet God knows through His foreknowledge that he will accept Christ and be a child of God was "selected from before the foundations of the world." Therefore there is a sense in which he is already in Christ as well, even though the benefits of that reality are not his to enjoy yet. Therefore, there is a sense in which we all are gathered together in one, in Christ now.

In God's kingdom, earthly time disappears. God sees past, present, and future as present realities. We, as believers, are the Church and the Church is of heavenly origin. We are not the Church because we obey Christ's teachings or prayed a certain prayer or sign our name on the rolls of a church. We are the Church because we are the body of Christ. Jesus said, *"No one has ascended to heaven but He who came down from heaven, that is, the Son of Man who is in heaven."* (John 3:13)
How could Jesus say, *"the Son of Man who **is** in heaven"* when he was sitting on earth talking with a man about heavenly realities?

 He spoke of us through the apostle Paul, *"..and raised us up together, and made us sit together in the heavenly places in Christ Jesus,"* (Eph.2:6)

These things might be a little confusing for some but understand that these are not essentials but understanding how God operates in space and time can help us understand how He works in us, His people, in regard to healing. When the Father raised Jesus from the dead, He saw us in Him, even then, and we were raised up from death with Him. Although we cannot see ourselves anywhere but here on planet earth with our natural senses, we are, never the less, seated together with Him. In heaven there is no sickness. Therefore, because of our position in Him, no sickness has any authority or right to exist in us any more than it has a right to exist in Christ.

Why do we take the Lord's Supper? If you ask many believers, even ministers, why they take the Lord's Supper their first answer is a begrudging, "Because Jesus told us to." This is a good enough reason in itself but it is not the full story. Eating the Lord's Supper was the primary reason for the assembly of the believers in the first two centuries of the Church. They understood the power of the covenant meal. The believers not only took the bread and wine but they ate a communal meal. This meal was called the agape (the love feast) it served as a reminder to the believers, first of their covenant relationship with the Lord but also of the fact that the same covenant bound them in relationship with one another in the local body.

Note how Luke speaks of the believers gathering together.

"Now on the first day of the week, when the disciples came together to break bread, Paul, ready to depart the next day, spoke to them and continued his message until midnight." (ACT 20:7)

"So continuing daily with one accord in the temple, and breaking bread from house to house, they ate their food with gladness and simplicity of heart, praising God and having favor with all the people. And the Lord added to the church daily those who were being saved." (ACT 2:46 ,47)

It is evident that the covenant meal was the center and focal point of the gathering. In the late first and early second century writings, the covenant meal was call the *"eucharistesas" or "the thanksgiving"* a sacrifice of thanksgiving for all the gifts of God, especially for the **"unspeakable gift," Jesus Christ**. By some of the fathers of the second century, the term was sometimes applied to the consecrated elements. The prayer of thanksgiving cited in, The Didache or, "The Teaching of the Twelve Apostles" is, for the cup first, *"We give thanks to Thee, our Father, for the holy vine of David Thy servant, which Thou hast made known to us through Jesus, Thy servant: to Thee be the glory forever." And for the bread: "We give thanks to Thee, our Father, for the life and knowledge which Thou hast made known to us through Jesus Thy servant: to Thee be the glory forever. As this broken bread was scattered upon the mountains and, gathered together, became one, so let Thy Church be gathered together from the ends of the earth into Thy Kingdom, for Thine is the glory and the power through Jesus Christ forever."* The believers prayed for the visible manifestation of that which was already manifested in the spirit, that the Church would be united as one in Christ.

In most evangelical and Pentecostal congregations today, the Lord's Supper is added on to the meeting at the end and usually rushed through. It is given little importance and little or no time is given to meditate upon the elements and their significance. Watchmen Nee, the Chinese apostle explains that the breaking of bread was so important to the believers in China that they had special meetings called "breaking of bread meetings" in which everything, including the worship and the teaching was directed toward the fact of the covenant meal. If any of the faithful members were unable to attend the meeting, the elders would send the elements with another church member who lived near that believer and they would go by their house and serve them the supper and pray for them.

As believers in the 21st century we need to reconsider the importance of the Lord's Supper to us today.

Where believers are taught to approach **the Lord's Table** with reverence and faith, expecting results, often the sick go away from the table healed. This is a common occurrence in such churches. We would do well to study the biblical material on **the covenant meal** and set ourselves to take it often and with faith toward receiving more from God through this means.

CHAPTER THIRTEEN

RECEIVING HEALING FOR YOURSELF

Once you have read over the preceding part of this book and studied the related Scriptures thoroughly, you should be able to come to the place where you truly believe that the healing power of God is for today and for you now. If you still battle serious doubts after that, you need to continue to study the Scripture on the subject until faith comes. There are some people who have received healing without a consciousness of personal faith, even unbelievers sometimes receive healing in the gospel meeting. We will discuss this later but right now I want to talk about how God has called believers to receive healing for themselves.

Many times a sick believer will go to a gospel meeting and have hands laid on him or receive prayer in some form and be healed. This is wonderful and we praise God for it. However, all a sick person really learns by being prayed for in a gospel meeting and receiving healing is, first, that God heals and secondly, when he gets sick again he needs to go back to another gospel meeting and be prayed for. Sometimes this is quiet effective. We need to hear from God as to how to proceed in these matters. At times God will move us to seek prayer from others and sometimes He might move you to just deal directly with Him regarding your healing and not receive prayer from others. God wants us to learn how to receive healing for ourselves by covenant, and not by gifts of healings or workings of miracles. That's why these gifts actually tend to work better for unbelievers or people who do not come from churches that believe in healing than they do for believers who come from churches that already believe in and practice healing. The gifts are primarily designed by God for us to use for others than ourselves.

(1) STUDY & MEDITATION

If you need healing, you should begin to pour over the promises of God in both Old and New Testaments and especially the gospel record, (Matthew, Mark, Luke and John) and saturate yourself with God's word. ***"Faith comes by hearing, and hearing by the word of God."***

If you spend quality time in God's word, even the way you think will change. You'll begin to think like God thinks. You will begin to talk like God talks and do things that God does. It will become part of your inner workings, part of who you are.

(2) CONFESSION: Confess all known sin and ask God to search your heart for any unconfessed sin that you might've forgotten. It is important to come to God with a clean heart.

(3) THANKSGIVING: Begin to think of things that God has done in your life that you can be thankful for and begin to thank God for them and everything that He has done, every blessing you have received, no matter how small. For many believers their prayer time is a complaint session with God about what they do not have. God responds much better to thanksgiving than He does a complaining heart. On the other hand, don't make the mistake that some do of thanking God for things the enemy has done. There are some who give thanks to God for sickness or tragedies, for all kinds of bad things that happen in their life. I realize that the Scriptures say,

"..giving thanks always for all things to God the Father in the name of our Lord Jesus Christ," (Ephesians 5:20) But the Greek word **huper**, here translated, "for" really should be translated "over" or "above" which makes a lot more sense. I think it's an insult to thank God for things that the devil has done. Having an attitude of thanksgiving is an important Christian virtue that needs to be developed in each of our lives.

(4) APPROPRIATION: Find all the promises of God that you can that have to do with healing and begin to meditate on them and quote them out loud in your devotion time. When you hear yourself speaking God's word things will begin to change.

(5) RECEIVING: Ask God in faith for healing on the basis of His promises.
"Therefore I say to you, all things for which you pray and ask, believe that you have received them, and they will be granted you." (Mark 11:24 NAS) much of unanswered prayer can be attributed to praying without first believing. Jesus said that when you pray you should believe that you **have received** the things you pray for. Some translations say, *"..believe that you will receive.."* but the original text actually uses the past tense. *"believe that you have received them and you will have them."*

The apostle John said, *"Now this is the confidence that we have in Him, that if we ask anything according to His will, He hears us. And if we know that He hears us, whatever we ask, we know that we have the petitions that we have asked of Him.* (1John 5:14-15)

What an amazing promise! If we pray according to His will He hears us and if He hears us we know that we have the answer. So we can say, if we pray according to His will we have the answer. So how do we know that we are praying according to His will? We simply make sure we are praying according to the book, the Holy Bible. If you look in the front page of your Bible it says "THE HOLY BIBLE, OLD AND NEW TESTAMENTS." What is a testament? If a person goes to an attorney to make out a will, this document called a "will" contain his wishes as to what should be done with the property or money that he leaves behind after his death. It is called formally a WILL AND TESTAMENT. It is called such because it is a **testament** or testimony of what that person's **will** is.

No sane person would make out a will and include in it things that were not his will to happen. It is a type of covenant.

That's why we find places where God promised things and we pray according to those promises so we can pray according to his will.

"For where there is a testament, there must also of necessity be the death of the testator. For a testament is in force after men are dead, since it has no power at all while the testator lives."
        (Hebrews 9:16,17)

Healing, then, is **God's WILL** for his children.

(6) PATIENCE
Whenever we ask for something from God in prayer, answers do not always come instantly. Many believers give up if they don't receive immediate answers to prayer

115

and assume that it wasn't God's will to do whatever it was they asked. Just because there is a delay between prayer and the visible answer does not mean that it is not God's will to answer that prayer. We must be prepared to exercise patience along with our faith in order to see the answer and receive what we desire from God. The New Testament word translated patience is *hupomone*, Vine's dictionary says it means, "an abiding under" (hupo, "under," meno, "to abide"), is almost invariably rendered "patience." I like to call patience hyper-continuing, in other words, continuing to do what you know is right to do regardless of the outcome yet with confidence that you will eventually achieve your goal. Many people think that when it comes to spiritual matters, somehow they should all take place instantly and without effort but that is simply not true. We learn to walk in faith through trial and error and many attempts that don't always work out perfectly. If we keep pressing forward we learn more and more and achieve better results. If we give up, we achieve nothing.

The apostle Paul exhorts us in many places to exercise patience along with our faith in order to inherit the promises.

"Rejoicing in hope, patient in tribulation, continuing steadfastly in prayer;" (Rom. 12:12)

*"Strengthened with all might, according to His glorious power, for all **patience** and longsuffering with joy; 12 giving thanks to the Father who has qualified us to be partakers of the inheritance of the saints in the light."*
(Col. 1:11,12)

The writer of Hebrews does the same, using Abraham as an example:
"*And so, after he had **patiently** endured, he obtained the promise.*" (Heb. 6:15)

The apostle James tells us how we obtain patience,
"*..knowing that the testing of your faith **produces patience**. But let patience have its perfect work, that you may be perfect and complete, lacking nothing.*"
(Jam. 1:3)

Jesus himself, speaking to one of the seven churches of Asia says,
"*To the angel of the church of Ephesus write, 'These things says He who holds the seven stars in His right hand, who walks in the midst of the seven golden lampstands: 'I know your works, your labor, your **patience**, and that you cannot bear those who are evil. And you have tested those who say they are apostles and are not, and have found them liars; "and you have persevered and have **patience**, and have labored for My name's sake and have not become weary.*"
(Rev. 2:1-3)

Jesus also commends the church at Thyatira for having patience in the midst of difficult circumstances. He doesn't promise us freedom from difficulties, tribulations, and distress; but sickness is a different category and He does promise us deliverance from sickness.

(7) PEACE
2Tim. 2:24-26; "*And a servant of the Lord must not quarrel but be gentle to all, able to teach, patient, 25 in humility correcting those who are in opposition, if God perhaps will grant them repentance, so that they may know*

117

the truth, 26 and that they may come to their senses and escape the snare of the devil, having been taken captive by him to do his will."

Many Christians, even some who have been believers for many years, never seem to learn to walk in peace. It is extremely important if we intend to walk in divine health to learn that no matter what our outward circumstances are, to stay in peace. Paul says that the servant of the Lord must not be quarrelsome. There are sometimes things that require a firm answer but often we fail to sense where the Holy Spirit is, on some question that we are dealing with. When I first began to get a hold of these teachings on healing, I was very zealous and wanted everybody to hear about them. When people would bring up controversial issues, if it was something that I was passionate about, I would argue with them for hours trying to convince them of the truth. What I didn't realize was that sometimes people are not willing to listen and that the Holy Spirit might want me to pray for them, rather than get into an argument about the Scriptures. Most of the time debate never really accomplishes anything except to get people upset.

Walking in peace requires that we refrain from contention, debate and the desire to convince people of the truth of our personal opinion. Another thing that I didn't realize at that juncture in my life was that often the person I was trying to convince of some great truth was in a position of authority greater than mine in the body of Christ. I needed to respect the authority and not contradict him especially in a contentious manner. That does not mean that I necessarily have to embrace what they are saying and agree with them but I need to respect their level of authority and cannot argue with them.

CHAPTER FOURTEEN

MINISTERING TO THE SICK

There are various biblical means that can be employed to minister the power of God to one needing healing.

1. Laying on of hands:
Mark 16:18 *"they will take up serpents; and if they drink anything deadly, it will by no means hurt them; they will lay hands on the sick, and they will recover."*

The first mention of the laying on of hands in the New Testament is found in Matthew's gospel 8:3; "Then Jesus put out His hand and touched him, saying, 'I am willing; be cleansed.' And immediately his leprosy was cleansed."
The act of laying on of hands, for healing or deliverance is mentioned approximately 21 times in the New Testament; (Mat. 8:3; 9:18,25; Mar. 1:31,41; 5:23,41; 6:5; 7:32-35; Luke 4:40; 5:13; 5:13; 8:23-25,54; 9:14-29; 13:10-21; Acts 3:7-10; 4:30; 5:12; 9:12;)
The laying on of hands is the most common method of healing mentioned in the New Testament. Believers are commanded by Jesus, Himself, to lay hands on the sick and expect them to recover. Any Christian church that does not practice ministry to the sick is not a true New Testament church. I have found the laying on of hands to be the most effective means to minister to sick people.

Laying hands on sick people helps them to release their faith, especially after having received teaching from the Bible along those lines. The teaching of the Word builds people up in their faith to receive healing but when someone that is anointed by the Holy Spirit, lays hands on them, they feel the power of the Spirit enter their bodies and it becomes much easier for them to receive the healing that they need.

Many people view the laying on of hands as a symbolic act but do not understand that, when one lays hands on someone in faith, there can be genuine transmission of power from the believer who is praying to the person who is receiving. When you lay hands on a sick person you should always believe that God's power is administered to them, regardless of whether you feel anything or whether you don't. Feeling really has very little to do with it. Often I have laid hands on someone and felt absolutely nothing and later found out that they were healed of some very serious ailments. Other times I have felt the flow of the Holy Spirit in great power surging out of my hands. Sometimes the person has fallen to the floor and been visibly impacted by the power of the Spirit, only to find out later that they were not healed. Healing is a matter of faith not of feeling.

Mark 6:4-6; *"But Jesus said to them, 'A prophet is not without honor except in his own country, among his own relatives, and in his own house.' 5 Now He could do no mighty work there, except that He laid His hands on a few sick people and healed them. 6 And He marveled because of their unbelief. Then He went about the villages in a circuit, teaching."*

Imagine that, in His own hometown, it says that Jesus could do no mighty work. We have always had the idea that Jesus could heal anybody, at anytime in anyplace, but apparently that is not the case. The apparent reason for this was the unbelief of the people in His town. However, even in that atmosphere of unbelief Jesus was able to get a few sick folks healed. The word "sick" in the above text means literally, lack of strength indicating that the people who were healed were sick with minor ailments. No lepers would be cleansed, nobody would receive their sight, no other major miracles. Why? Because of their unbelief. They did not accept Jesus or who He said He was.

I have found that even in the worst of situations, most of the time, I have been able to get at least a few people healed through the laying on of hands.

2. Anointing with oil:
Mark 6:13 *And they cast out many demons, and anointed with oil many who were sick, and healed them.*

Another common method of healing practiced in the Bible is the anointing with oil.
The command and the promise.
James 5:14-16; *Is anyone among you sick? Let him call for the elders of the church, and let them pray over him,* **anointing him with oil in the name of the Lord***. 15 And the prayer of faith will save the sick, and the Lord will raise him up. And if he has committed sins, he will be forgiven. 16 Confess your trespasses to one another, and pray for one another, that you may be healed. The effective, fervent prayer of a righteous man avails much."*

Here, the apostle James commands the elders of the church to anoint the sick with oil and pray the prayer of faith over them, expecting them to be healed. Anointing the sick with oil seems to help people with weak faith to be able to receive healing from Christ. They feel the oil being smeared on their head and sometimes the physical feelings help them to release their faith. Also, believers who have been in sin and become sick because of the sin that they are involved in, sometimes need to come to the elders and confess their sins and receive the assurance from the elders that their sins are forgiven. They are anointed with oil and the prayer of faith is prayed. Very few churches practice this, perhaps because they don't want to appear to be like the Catholic Church. But we need to recognize that the New Testament commands us to practice this method. That does not mean that every time you sin, that you need to go to a priest or pastor and confess your sins to him. In cases of extreme sins, especially where the life of the church could be damaged through it, it will often help to confess your sins to another person, especially one who carries authority in the church before receiving prayer for healing.

3. Gifts of healing with word of knowledge:

Often in gospel meetings, ministers of God operate in the gifts of healings in conjunction with a word of knowledge. In other words, God will give them a word about someone in the audience who is sick with a certain disease. They will call out that disease until the person who has that sickness comes forward or just declare that they are healed. I can't really find a biblical example of this process but it seems to work and I have seen some amazing results by those who use that process. God uses different operations with the same gift. Kathryn Khulman who had one of the most powerful healing ministries of the twentieth century always employed this method.

4. The command of faith:

Mat. 8:5-13; *Now when Jesus had entered Capernaum, a centurion came to Him, pleading with Him, 6 saying, "Lord, my servant is lying at home paralyzed, dreadfully tormented." 7 And Jesus said to him, "I will come and heal him." 8 The centurion answered and said, "Lord, I am not worthy that You should come under my roof. But only speak a word, and my servant will be healed. 9 "For I also am a man under authority, having soldiers under me. And I say to this one, 'Go,' and he goes; and to another, 'Come,' and he comes; and to my servant, 'Do this,' and he does it." 10 When Jesus heard it, He marveled, and said to those who followed, "Assuredly, I say to you, I have not found such great faith, not even in Israel! 11 "And I say to you that many will come from east and west, and sit down with Abraham, Isaac, and Jacob in the kingdom of heaven. 12 "But the sons of the kingdom will be cast out into outer darkness. There will be weeping and gnashing of teeth." 13 Then Jesus said to the centurion, "Go your way; and as you have believed, so let it be done for you." And his servant was healed that same hour."*

There are numerous incidents in the Gospel record of Jesus healing people by a simple command like, "be healed," or some other similar command. He doesn't specifically instruct us to do the same but he does say, *"the works that I do shall you do also".* He also commands His disciples to heal the sick. In all the Gospel record there is not one incident where Jesus actually prayed for a sick person asking God the father, to heal them. He ministered to the sick in many different ways but never by actually praying a petitionary prayer for them. As you go through the book of Acts you will find the same pattern in effect. Paul, Peter, Ananias or any other person

125

mentioned in the book of Acts as ministering to the sick person, none of them actually prayed for one to be healed.

A classic example is where Peter and John were going up to the Temple at the hour of prayer. They found a crippled man there who asked for alms. Look at Peter's response:

"Silver and gold I do not have, but what I do have I give you: In the name of Jesus Christ of Nazareth, rise up and walk." 7 And he took him by the right hand and lifted him up, and immediately his feet and ankle bones received strength. 8 So he, leaping up, stood and walked and entered the temple with them - walking, leaping, and praising God." (Acts 3:6-8)

Peter said, *"... what I do have I give to you..."* If Peter would have been like many of us he would've said something like, "Well now, we don't really know what God is going to do, but we'll pray for you and if it's His will He will heal you." It's interesting that approaches like this are generally considered humble and realistic but none of the biblical record contains this type of praying. Those who minister to the sick, that we have a record of, always pray with confidence and boldness. It seems that they knew exactly what God was going to do.

5. Spontaneous healing:
What I call spontaneous healings are healings that take place without anybody doing anything particular and may not even know that the person is sick. I believe that these types of healings took place in the ministry of Jesus and the apostles, but just weren't recorded in the New Testament record. I have often been preaching in different places and had people come up after the meeting and tell me, that while they listened to the word

being preached, all the pain left their body and they were later able to determine that they were totally healed. I always expect these things to happen whenever I am teaching the Bible in different places.

6. The use of anointed cloths:
ACT 19:11,12; *Now God worked unusual miracles by the hands of Paul, so that even handkerchiefs or aprons were brought from his body to the sick, and the diseases left them and the evil spirits went out of them.*

There is no particular example of Jesus using cloths that are prayed over or have been in contact with His body for the healing of the sick; except for the woman with the hemorrhage that came and touched his clothes. (Mar. 5) There is no command to do so as there is with the laying on of hands but at least we have biblical examples of this principle and Paul's example. There are, also, various Old Testament uses of various articles that effected healing. In Second Kings 4:18-35; we see that Elisha instructed his servant Gehazi to take his walking stick and go ahead of him to the home of a woman whose child had died and to put the stick against the child's face. This he did and Elisha arrived later and the child revived. Also in Second Kings 13:20-24; a corpse of a brigand was thrown into Elisha's tomb to hide it and the man was raised from the dead.

We have often used cloths to pray over and send to people who were unable to attend a meeting. The first time we did that was in Chiapas Mexico. A man came to a meeting and asked us to come up to his village and pray for his wife who was dying from tuberculosis. The village was an hour's walk from there which would have added

127

three hours to our trip and caused us to miss the even meeting in a nearby city. We prayed and asked the Lord and He reminded me of that text in Acts 19. We prayed over the man's hat and instructed him to put it on his wife and pray over her in the name of Jesus. Six months later I found out that she had been completely healed three days after prayer. Since then we have used this means on many occasions and found some surprising results.

7. Unusual methods of healing:

Jesus ministered healing in some rather unusual ways. He sometimes spit in the eyes of blind persons. One time He spit in the dirt and made some mud with His spit, rubbed it into a blind man's eyes and told him to go to a certain pool and wash his eyes. After he did so the blind man was healed. I'll never forget the first time I ever did anything like that. I was preaching in a church in Tegucigalpa, Honduras. A young girl came up for healing who wore glasses as thick as the bottom part of a Coca-Cola bottle. The Lord told me to have her take her glasses off and after I said that, He told me to spit in her eyes and He would heal her. I wouldn't do it. I was embarrassed. I went ahead and prayed for her eyes and then asked her if she could see any better. She looked at me with kind of a disturbed look and said, "no." It almost seemed like she was aware that I had disobeyed God. I told her to come back the next night. She did, and came down again in the prayer line. Between last night and that time I had repented and made up my mind I would obey God even if it got me kicked out of the church. Again I asked her to take off her glasses. I spit on my fingers, rubbed it around and then slapped it in her eyes. And I asked her if she could see any better. She said, "no" but not with the same attitude as the night before. Obeying God had given me confidence and I said to her, "you soon will be." The following night she came back and I noticed that she didn't have the thick, coke bottle glasses on anymore. She came up and asked to testify and she said, "All of you know me and remember that I always wore these thick glasses and without them I could barely see a thing. But after prayer last night I began to see better." and with that she open her small print Bible and began to read from it with no glasses. The crowd went crazy in spontaneous worship, praising God for what He had done.

THE JOB BEFORE US

Personally, I have been praying for sick people for almost 35 years and I plan to continue doing so as long as I live on this earth. But I have also realized that I could pray for people 24 -7, for my entire life, and never really put a dent in the number of sick people that are on the earth. There are over 6 billion people on planet earth right now and I would guess that more than half of them are sick. Three billion sick people is a really conservative estimate because there are nations in which almost everybody is sick. So if three billion people on earth are sick, do you realize how many that is? If they all stood in a prayer line shoulder to shoulder they would stretch from Los Angeles to New York more than 500 times. If they lined up at the equator they would circle the globe more than 68 times. If you only prayed for each one for only five seconds, it would still take 475 years to pray for all of them. I think you get the picture, it's the impossible job. So what do we do? We have to think in terms of multiplication. There are over 400 million spirit filled Christians on the face of the earth. If we could train even half of them to pray for the sick, it would only require each one to pray for 15 sick people to get the job done.

Training and releasing people to do the work is the only solution to the problem.

SIGNS AND WONDERS and the expansion of the kingdom

The entire story of the church in its initial years, as told in the book of Acts, is filled with signs, wonders, unusual miracles, gifts of the Spirit. The only chapters in the book where miracles didn't occur are the chapters that tell of church controversy and problems. There is not the slightest hint or suggestion that these supernatural manifestations were scheduled to pass away.

In his book entitled, Look Out The Pentecostals Are Coming, Peter Wagner, who at that time was a missionary in South America, and part of a denomination that did not believe in the present day manifestations of the Holy Spirit, began to notice that, while the church he pastored and other evangelical churches grew only marginally and with great difficulty, the Pentecostal congregations nearby were growing exponentially. He began an investigation in an attempt to determine why these congregations were growing so successfully. He came up with many natural reasons, like the worship songs which were more culturally-relevant, the emotion charged preaching and other factors. Finally he realized that all those factors weren't enough to account for the difference in the growth rates of different congregations. Looking deeper into this situation and interviewing believers and pastors, he realized that the reason for the growth among the Pentecostals was due to the manifestation of the Holy

Spirit in their midst. My years of working among the people in Spanish-speaking countries, has revealed the same thing. Almost all the people I have spoken with and ask for their testimonies, have said that there were undeniably miracles that caused them to turn to Christ from dead religion.

Once I was preaching the word in a town in Mexico called Xicotepec. In the Aztec language" tepec" means hill and "xico" means wasp, therefore Xicotepec means wasp hill. Just in case someone asks you. Anyway, I preached several nights in a church there which had about eighty members. Most of the people were workers in the coffee plantations. The last night that I preached some people brought a man who was totally blind. After the preaching, he came forward for prayer, led by one of his friends. After laying hands on him I asked him if he could see anything. He looked around and said yes. I pointed to the clock on the wall and said, "What's that?" He replied, "It's a clock." Then I asked, "What time is it?" The man looked again and told us the correct time. At that moment a wave of the Holy Spirit descended in the building and it seemed that everyone began weeping all at once. About a year later I was back at that church again. They were meeting in a different building and there were about four hundred people in the opening service. After the meeting I asked the pastor how the church had grown so quickly. He said that it was the blind man you prayed for the last time you were here. He explained that the man who had received his sight owned a store in the center of town. He used to sit in a rocking chair in front of his store and talk to people passing by. Sometimes he had a young boy with him who would lead him by the hand so that he could take a walk around the neighborhood. Everyone knew this man and knew that he was blind. The morning after he was healed he took a walk around the neighborhood by himself, without the boy. He tried to speak with some of the people in the neighboring stores but they became terrified and thought he was a ghost. Some of them shut their stores and put a closed sign in their window. After a few days, people realized that he was not a ghost and that an extraordinary miracle had taken place. People with needs began to come to that church and within six months it grew to nearly four hundred people.

Another example of signs and wonders evangelism that I like to tell took place in Phnom Penh, Cambodia. I was preaching in a church there and met a man named Mr. Chun. I had heard that he had been raised from the dead and was curious to hear his whole story. One of the brothers who spoke English took me to Mr. Chun's house and fortunately, I took my video camera with me and was able to video his story and his wife's story. His wife had been a believer only about two weeks, when Mr. Chun became very sick and after a couple of days he died. His wife and children were grieving and the Buddhist neighbors came over and tried to console her. Since she had no money for a cremation, they took some of the boards from the wooden shack that they lived in and built a rustic coffin for Mr. Chun.

Then they left her alone with him. She tried to lift the body and put it into the coffin but by this time rigor mortis had set in and the body was stiff. She was unable to get him into the coffin. She laid him back down on the floor and began to weep out of frustration. Without really knowing why, she took her Bible and laid it open on Mr.

Chun's chest and began to pray. She said, "Lord, it is not fair that my husband died without having a chance to hear your word and to receive Jesus as his savior. Please give my husband a chance to hear your word." Just then, Mr. Chun's eyes began to move and he sat upright suddenly. He said to his wife, "give me some rice, I'm hungry." After eating some rice he sent his wife off to the church and said, "Go find that pastor and tell him to come down here and show me how to get saved. I still feel sick and I might die again and if I do I don't want to go back to that same place I was just at, so hurry and bring the pastor back here." Mr. Chun received Jesus and was soon quite well but the whole neighborhood had seen him dead and just like in Mexico, they thought he was a ghost and shut their doors and hid inside when he would walk by. Gradually the people began to accept the **miracle** that had happened and inquire about what power had caused this mighty occurrence to happen. Within a few months over forty people had come to the Lord and Mr. Chun pastors a house church that meets in his shack.

The same boards that were nailed together to make his coffin are now back forming part of his wall in the wooden shack that he lives in. The story is much longer than this. I could tell you about Mr. Chun seeing the lake of fire and what happened to him before his wife's prayers caused his spirit to be sent back into his body so that he might be saved. Remember that Mrs. Chun was only about two weeks old in the Lord when she **raised her husband from the dead** who had been dead for fourteen hours. If you are a young Christian or whatever state you are in, don't let Satan convince you that you can't minister to the sick, or even raise somebody from the dead. Actually, the only people I know of and where I have been able to verify that someone has been raised from the dead, are ones that have been raised up by people who were not in full-time ministry and most of them, young Christians.

HOW TO GET STARTED

The first thing that happened with me was that the Lord put a strong desire in my heart to see miracles and to move in the supernatural gifts of the Spirit. But with others, God has done different things. I know pastors who didn't believe in healing, who didn't want healing in their churches and God began to heal people, while they were preaching even though they didn't want healing to happen. They didn't want the Holy Spirit coming in rocking the boat. God does things His way and doesn't have to ask permission.

If you have a desire to see the sick healed, that's a good thing. First Corinthians 14:1 says, "*Pursue love, and desire spiritual gifts..*" The word" desire" in that sentence is a very strong word in the Greek language. It means to be extremely passionate about something. If you're passionate about seeing healing and miracles, you are a good candidate to see some of them. What I suggest is, every time you see somebody that needs healing, you offer to pray for them unless the Holy Spirit tells you not to. Any time you're around people, begin to ask Jesus to show you what their needs are. God will often give you a word about somebody's situation or He may even cause you to feel pain in your body that is not actually your pain. You feel the pain of the other person who needs healing. You may be near somebody who has a pain in their back and all of a sudden your back starts hurting, maybe not very strongly but enough to let you know that something is going on. Then you can ask that person if they have something wrong with their back and if they do, offer to pray for them in the name of Jesus. Lay hands on them and expect the power of God to flow out of your hands and into their body and bring total healing. If they get healed, that will give you an opportunity to talk to them about Jesus and His mercy and love toward them. If they don't get healed, don't get discouraged. Many times healings actually manifest later or the person may experience a slight change; maybe their pain level will diminish some and they may be encouraged to pray themselves. I have often found that people who I pray for, who experienced no particular change at the time, or maybe only a slight change, later found that they were totally healed.

It's time for believers to get over the idea that praying for the sick is something that only professional ministers are supposed to do. **Jesus said that signs would follow them that believe**. He didn't put any other qualifications on the line, except believing.

Signs and wonders have never been done away with. They should be part of the normal day-to-day operation of the church today. The problem is that the church today, for the most part, has not really believed that these things are available to us today. I want to encourage you to press in, to believe God, to study the Scriptures on this subject and to step out in faith and **expect the sick to be healed, expect miracles to happen, expect Jesus to do mighty works and He will.**

APPENDIX I

A CALL TO INTEGRITY

There are a growing number, mostly radio preachers, especially in the USA who specialize in "heresy hunting." They listen to the sermons and read the books by anyone who moves in the power of God and attempt to find some error in their teachings and then, attempt to destroy these ministers through slander and calumnies. Admittedly, they often don't need to fabricate anything, in order to come up with some critique that titillates the ears of the carnal hearers. These preachers make a handsome living through donations that come from fearful listeners and those who read their books. However, the other side of the coin is that the ones who are being criticized are often, outside the bounds of scripture and are coming up with new fanciful ideas that have little, or no value to the hearers, but only cause the unwary to think that the preacher is really intelligent and very anointed. These self appointed "doctrine police" are like Nebuchadnezzar whom God used to punish Israel when they were in disobedience. Of course, God later judged Nebuchadnezzar.

Some ministers have caused a bad name to the healing and deliverance ministry by using unscriptural practices like selling bottles of "anointed oil" and anointed prayer cloths, holy water from the Jordan River, and Salt from the Dead Sea. Desperate people are often caught up in the hype of these preachers and have been known to even borrow money to send donations to them.

As Al Houghton clearly stated, "There is a major difference between what happened in Acts 19 and what is advertised in some cases today. The difference is Paul never sent his handkerchief with a return envelope, telling people to immediately send back their best love gift! Paul's motivation was pure. I am not so sure about some of those I see today."[14]

A large number of ministers base their ministries on a gift and not on the word of God. They seem to move in great power for a time and then seem to drift into strange doctrines and extra-scriptural beliefs and practices or fall into sin.

One preacher well known for his healing ministry, I heard say that Adam, because he had dominion could fly. He further explained that in order to exercise the dominion that God had given him, he could transport himself to the moon just by a thought. Another, is now famous for taking people on trips to the third heaven. He claims to have conversed with the Apostle Paul on one of his trips. He is known to conduct groups of people on out of body experiences, or third heaven visitations, by having them all lie on the floor with their heads touching in the middle, arranged like the spokes of a wheel. This is nothing more than a slightly modified form of Boko-maru, a new age occultic practice.

Paul speaks, in Second Corinthians twelve, about his own visit to the third heaven. He says first that there would be no profit in bragging about it and the content of what

---

[14] Houghton, Al; Purifying the Altar; (1990 edition) P. 41. A must read, self published and available only from www.wordatwork.org

happened was of such a holy nature that he would not speak about it. Yet, ministers today spend time bragging about all their spiritual experiences.

All these "out there" teachings do no good for needy people .They are skillfully designed to make the listener think that he is part of something new and unique and that this preacher really has "the stuff." There are few preachers out there today who don't use these same methods at least to some degree.

Dr. Sam Storms, in his study on 2Cor. 12; says, "Let us never lose sight of the fact that the primary reason Paul mentioned his heavenly translation was to provide a context for understanding his "thorn in the flesh," his *weakness* about which he is happy to boast (11:30). Paul wants to draw attention to this 'thorn' and its purpose in subduing his prideful heart. In such obvious weakness, together with insults, hardships, persecutions, and calamities he will be content and "boast all the more gladly"

I have never heard one of these high-powered ministers brag about their weaknesses like Paul did.

THE SIMPLE GOSPEL
As ministers of the gospel of Christ we need to keep our gospel simple enough for the unlearned among us to be able to understand it. When I was in seminary in Southern California I was teaching a mid week Bible class for the church. A man who worked doing janitorial work for the church, I will call Billy began to come to my class. Billy was somewhat challenged in the intellectual department but loved Jesus and had simple faith in him.

At the same time, I was studying Bible Greek and Systematic Theology. As I studied, my teaching became more and more spiced up with Greek and Hebrew words. After one of my teachings, which I thought was particularly good, the Lord spoke to me on the way home saying, "Do you think Billy understood your teaching tonight?" I cringed at the thought of what would come next. Jack Deere said "The omniscient one never asks questions in order to obtain information." I finally answered, "No Lord, I don't think so." "Then you have made me a respecter of persons, you must make your messages simple enough for Billy to understand." We need to stay with the Scriptures, chapter and verse. The more I spend time in the Gospels, meditating in the teachings of Jesus, the more I am astounded by how simple, yet profound they are.

CHARACTER AND CONDUCT BEFORE CHARISMA

Many, in healing ministries, falsify the numbers and facts regarding people saved and healed in their meetings. This is so common that preachers call stretching the numbers being "evang-elastic", and laugh about it.

False prophets abound in many places. The most prominent of them all, who could often tell people that he called out in a meeting, their name, what disease they had, and other pertinent facts about them, was later caught in the parking lot of a nationally known ministry, to which he was related, stumbling drunk and making sexual advances toward young boys. Another, almost as well respected as a prophet, was caught using his prophetic gifting to solicit sexual favors from women he had ministered to. Many of them have prophesied major events and catastrophes over and over again, that didn't come to pass and few have said a word about it. One prominent Southern California pastor said that Jesus would return by 1981, and said if it didn't happen he would quit the ministry. He is quite old now but has denied that he ever said it. When a true believer ignores the discerning of the Holy Spirit, (usually determined by a sense of discomfort in his spirit) and decides to follow a false prophet, he grieves the Holy Spirit. After a few times of grieving the Spirit, His voice begins to get dimmer and dimmer until one cannot hear His voice, hardly at all. This is a dangerous place to be. Don't ignore the discerning of the Spirit that operates within you.

THE MAMMON ISSUE
Churches, without batting an eye, charge money for conferences and staunchly defend the practice. Some of these at the same time operate ministries to the poor and see no contradiction in the fact that the same poor who stop by for a bag of groceries at the church, cannot afford to attend one of their pricey conferences and feel unwelcome at the church meetings.

A large percentage of the leaders of larger ministries, live opulent lifestyles, own multi-million dollar mansions, drive fancy cars and are "believing God" for their own jet airplanes, if they don't already own one. One, the son of the senior leader of an east coast ministry, saw a house he liked while on a trip in Scotland. He bought the house and had it disassembled and shipped to the USA and re-assembled there at the cost of one million dollars, not counting the house. I'm not suggesting that we should take vows of poverty, but many of us need to adopt a more moderate lifestyle and use what is left over for the extension of the kingdom of God in poorer nations.

Recently a nationally known healing "revivalist" said in a meeting that there were in that meeting, a thousand people who God was touching to give a thousand dollars in the offering. He claimed that God told him if they would obey and give the thousand dollars that God would return it a thousand fold. When confronted by some of his friends, concerning the unscriptural nature of his statement, he admitted that he had not really heard from the Lord but in the meeting never recanted his story. A few weeks later he was discovered to be living a double life in an adulterous affair, he resigned from his ministry and filed for divorce.

The bottom line is the love of money, self-aggrandizement and pride.

We need to consider our motivations for the home we live in, the automobile we drive and the clothes we wear. Who are we trying to impress, God? Not hardly! His house makes any of ours look like an outdoor toilet!

I am convinced that if every believer would only give into the ministries that God tells him to give into, that a large number of churches and ministries would go broke in a short time. I believe that day is coming when believers will wake up and realize that they are being taken for a ride and begin to ignore and refuse to give their hard earned money to churches and ministries like these. Then the situation will change over night! The problem is that as P.T. Barnum, the circus magnet, is reported to have said, "A sucker is born every minute."

A TV preacher was discovered to have been using an in-ear radio connection, where his wife, who had previously spoken with people who told her their problem, and then, giving him that information about those persons. Immediately following, the preacher would speak out words of knowledge, and call them up for healing prayer. After he was exposed for having bamboozled the people, he was confronted and admitted to the allegations, but said it helped the people to have more faith.

Manipulation and control abound especially in finances. Few pastors and ministers today pay attention to Jesus' admonition in Luke 16:11 *"Therefore if you have not been faithful in the unrighteous mammon, who will commit to your trust the true riches? and if you have not been faithful in what is another man's, who will give you what is your own? No servant can serve two masters; for either he will hate the one and love the other, or else he will be loyal to the one and despise the other. You cannot serve God and mammon."*

The issue of "Mammon"[15] is one of the pivotal issues of our day. Ministers who misrepresent, misuse or obtain money under false pretenses are on dangerous ground.

TITLES
Others have begun to adopt special titles of Apostle, Prophet, Bishop, or Doctor. Some of the same would criticize the Catholics for calling their priests "Father" without considering that Jesus was not coming against a few specific titles but against all self-exaltation. Look at what he said.
"Do not call anyone on earth your father; for one is your Father, He who is in heaven. And do not be called teachers; for one is your Teacher, the Christ. But he who is greatest

---

[15] Treasure and wealth personified and opposed to God.

143

among you shall be your servant. And whoever exalts himself will be abased, and he who humbles himself will be exalted. (Mat. 23:9-12)

It's time for ministers to realize that God is not an aging and somewhat senile grandfather, who smiles at the recalcitrance of His grandchildren. God is a consuming fire! There will be a day of reckoning and it will begin at the house of God. We ministers must take heed and repent before it is too late. We will be held to a higher standard.

A famous healing evangelist of the fifties was asked by one of his disciples, "How do you know when it's time to move on to another town." The evangelist replied, "When you take the people by the ankles and shake em good and all that falls out of their pockets is small change, then it's time to move on." That same evangelist although he possessed extraordinary giftings in healings and miracles was found dead in the Jack Tar Hotel on the waterfront in San Francisco. The cause of death was alcohol poisoning.

Another healing evangelist of the earlier generation of healing evangelists was heard to say, at the peak of his fame. "Almost the entire world is at my feet to worship me." This minister also possessed a powerful working of gifts of healing and miracles especially for rheumatoid arthritis. Hopelessly twisted up cripples would be totally healed in his meetings. A short time after the declaration mentioned above, he began to experience symptoms of the same disease he was known for healing so many of. Later when Lester Sumrall visited him he found the evangelist in a wheel chair in an almost totally paralyzed condition with,--yes you guessed it—rheumatoid arthritis. Just because judgment doesn't come immediately doesn't mean that it won't come eventually. God's mercy causes him to hold off judgment for a time. But....

"Do not be deceived, God is not mocked; for whatever a man sows, that he will also reap." (Galatians 6:7)

It is imperative for believers to cultivate the discerning of spirits within them and to pay attention to the inner workings of the Spirit of God, in their spirit. Believers often make excuses in their hearts for the obvious ego trips that ministers are on. It is so common that most of us take it as normal. If believers would seriously pray about their giving and refuse to support ministries that exhibit unbiblical lifestyles in dress, possessions, homes, automobiles, indulge in flagrant fundraising techniques and would refuse to give a nickel to those ministries, they would dry up over night and God would raise up ones who were more concerned about character than charisma, morality than money and simplicity rather than sensationalism.

SOME TRUE KINGDOM ADVANCING MINISTRIES

I have tended to dwell on the negative in this chapter but the truth is that there are many bright spots on the scene both, in past and present, who have set sterling examples of great faith, with humility and integrity to go with it.

William Joseph Seymour, (1870-1922)

An African American preacher, founder of the Azusa Street Mission in Los Angeles and the Father of the Pentecostal movement.
Seymour was born the son of freed slaves in Centerville, Louisiana and studied at a Bible school founded by Charles Parham in Houston, TX in 1905. He went to

145

California and preached the infilling of the Holy Spirit with speaking in tongues. He began the Azusa Street Mission in 1906, after the outpouring of the Holy Spirit that began just before that, on Bonnie Brae St. That outpouring went non-stop for three years, extended to nations all over the world and broke down racial barriers. Healing power was poured out to such an extent that people were often healed in the street, after coming within a couple of blocks of the mission. Seymour is one of my greatest heroes, most notably because he was so heavily persecuted and slandered and yet refused to lash out at his critics.

John Graham Lake, (1870-1935)
Another, from the early twentieth century is John G. Lake, a Canadian who received the baptism of the Holy Spirit in 1907 in the wake of the Azusa Street Revival and became known for his ministry as a missionary and "faith healer." Lake went by faith to South Africa in 1908 with a small team. They established more than five hundred churches in five years and then Lake returned to the USA. He settled in Spokane Washington where he established the "Healing Rooms" ministry where it was said in the secular press that over one hundred thousand documented miracles had occurred in five years. Lake preached the gospel in difficult times and circumstances, burying his first wife in So. Africa and in the same year a dozen of his workers died in their church planting effort, some because of malnutrition. Lake refused to compromise his stand of faith concerning the finances. His workers planted churches all over So. Africa. He never resorted to the fund raising tactics that became commonplace in later generations of healing ministry.

Fred Francis Bosworth (1877-1958)

F. F. Bosworth came into the fullness of the Holy Spirit in 1906 and from then on, preached the gospel for the remainder of his life. He was nearly beaten to death by an angry mob in Hearne, Texas in 1911 for preaching to a black congregation in a revival meeting.[16]

From 1920, he did large meetings in tents and auditoriums with an emphasis on healing and miracles through two generations of healing revivals. Although Bosworth had association with both, John Alexander Dowie and William Branham, he managed to stay out of the theatrics, ego trips, controversial doctrines, questionable financial practices and moral problems that plagued the healing evangelists of that period. In 1924, Bosworth published the first edition of *Christ the Healer*, a book that contains many of his sermons on the topic of faith healing and his responses to his critics. The book is still in print today. After 1951 Bosworth began to travel internationally, doing crusades in Africa, Europe, parts of Asia and the Caribbean.

According to his son, Robert, when the time came for Bosworth's homegoing, the family was gathered around his bedside talking, laughing, and singing, Bosworth then looked up, never saw the family members present, and began to greet and hug people - he was enraptured ... He did this for several hours, then with a smile on his face he laid back and went to sleep. I owe a great debt of gratitude to Fred Bosworth for his book, which contributed greatly to my early understanding of healing and also for the testimony of a "no nonsense" healing

---

[16] For more information on Bosworth see Wikapedia.com or http://en.believethesign.com/index.php?title=F.F._Bosworth> for a detailed account of his beating. This kind was not uncommon in the southern states.

ministry. He walked in a high level of integrity, free of the competitive spirit and full of the compassion of Christ through five decades of ministry.

Wayne Myers

One present day example is Wayne Myers of Mexico City who was a great source of inspiration to us in the early days of our ministry. After serving in the Navy during W.W.-II Wayne left his home in Mississippi for Mexico without any promised support. We knew that God was calling us to go out by faith to Mexico and that He had instructed us not to make our needs known to anyone, but we had never heard of a missionary who had lived by any similar commitment. We found later that Wayne had not only lived completely by faith but that he was accustomed to giving away large sums of money, often making pledges into offerings for the work of the Lord when he was totally broke. Over the years, millions of dollars have passed through his hands but he gives extravagantly into the works in many nations and continues to live in a modest house and live a lifestyle of moderation, except in giving. Wayne was influenced by the healing evangelists especially T.L. Osborne. Wayne traveled around Mexico extensively doing evangelistic and healing crusades. Like the apostles of old he has often been in dangerous situations. Once some brothers put him in the trunk of a car and snuck out of town, because an angry mob was coming to the church to kill him. He is better known, however, for his messages on "Faith giving and faith living." Wayne says, "He who lives to give will never live to lack." Wayne's influence on local churches in Mexico in the area of giving and trusting God to fill every need, is so widespread that it seems to have influenced the entire body of Christ in that nation. Instead of looking to churches in foreign nations to full their needs, these churches start trusting the God who has no limitations to supply their needs abundantly. The world needs more missionaries and ministries of every kind who walk in this level of integrity.

I could go on describing other powerful ministries that preached the gospel, moved in power and maintained strong integrity and humility, like my friends, Hugo and Celso Contreras of Argentina, apostolic founders of the Mission Cristiana y Missionera which has grown to hundreds of churches in South America. Also, my dear friend Nehemiah Lac, who has planted hundreds of house churches in Southeast Asia; He spent years in prison for preaching the gospel in his homeland of Vietnam. I have never known a man that carried such a marked anointing of peace. I also want to mention John Wimber, founder of the Vineyard movement, Kenneth E. Hagin, Lester Sumrall and (all of these, I was privileged to hear preach the word on several occasions). There are numerous others but I think these few examples demonstrate that God is not without testimony of power ministry functioning with deep integrity and humility.

APPENDIX II

A FURTHER LOOK AT CESSATIONISM

Cessationism is the belief in the ceasing of all miracles, healings and works of a supernatural character in the church after the close of the apostolic period. i.e. after the death of the apostle John.

First, there is no biblical evidence or even the suggestion that the supernatural power of God was to be removed from the Church at any time. The primary biblical text used to support this theory is, 1Cor.13:8-10; *"Love never fails. But whether there are prophecies, they will fail; whether there are tongues, they will cease; whether there is knowledge, it will vanish away. For we know in part and we prophesy in part. But when that which is perfect has come, then that which is in part will be done away."*

The cessationist argument goes like this: The statement, **"..that which is perfect..."** refers to the completion of the New Testament Scriptures, and at that point, **"...that which is in part..."** i.e. prophesies, tongues, miracles, and all things supernatural will pass away.

In order to understand this statement from the apostle Paul we need only to apply basic rules of Bible interpretation especially in this case the rule of context, which says that we must understand the statement from the larger context that it is found within. These basic rules of Bible interpretation are agreed upon by all evangelical scholars but sadly, when it is convenient, some tend to ignore them. So let's look at the larger context of the discussion, continuing in verse 12 *"For now we see in a mirror, dimly, but then face to face. Now I know in part, but then I shall know just as I also am known."* We ask the question, now that we have the New Testament do we know Christ "face to face"? Do we know Him even as He knows us? Of course not! These things will not take place until His appearing. Therefore, the supernatural aspect of the gospel will not pass away until His appearing, His second coming! At that time we will see Him face to face and know Him as we are known by Him.

Another passage used is Hebrews 2:3-4 *"How shall we escape, if we neglect so great salvation; which at the first began to be spoken by the Lord, and was confirmed unto us by them that heard him; God also bearing them witness, both with signs and wonders, and with divers miracles, and gifts of the Holy Ghost, according to his own will?"*
"The verses say that miracle signs were performed by "them" i.e. the apostles and not "us". The writer of Hebrews, being slightly later than the age of the Apostles, is witness to the events, but not participating in them any longer." This comment quoted above uses the King James Version without consulting the Greek which literally translated reads, *"...bearing witness with God by signs both and wonders..."*[17] "Them" is not found in the text and even if it was, the argument is rather flimsy.

The second verse, popular with cessationists, is Ephesians 2:20 which says, *"Having been built on the foundation of the apostles and prophets, Jesus Christ Himself being the chief cornerstone,"*

---

[17] Marshall, Alfred; Literal English Translation

The text is interpreted to read that apostles and prophets were only foundational to the church (and thus not continuing offices). This theory assumes that apostles and prophets were the only ones working miracles, which is clearly false. (see Acts 9:1-19) The text does not prove even, that the office of apostle or prophet have passed away, much less that healing and miracles were done away with, or with the passing of the last apostle, miracles performed through people, ceased. Some cessationists make reference to 1 Corinthians 13:8-10 as their main argument, though the majority of cessationists today do not feel that it can be used as an argument for cessationism.

Historical Evidence
Some Cessationists, e.g., Benjamin Warfield, argue that there has been no solid objective scientific reference of the working of miracles manifested within the mainstream church for the last nineteen centuries. References to miracles and spiritual gifts throughout church history, they claim, have been associated with cults and mystics. More recent studies, however, e.g., Foubister, Frost, Greer, Kelsey, Kydd, Ruthven, and Shogren, have shown that the evidence is much more positive than the citations offered by cessationists.

The following are examples drawn from documents of the early church fathers and historians. John Wimber says, "Signs and wonders did not cease with the close of the first century or with the completion of the canon. They have continued to occur in each of the three major historical periods (The time of the Church Fathers, the medieval period, and the time of the Reformation).

When the ones in authority endorsed the gifts, they occurred openly and widely within the church. When those in authority no longer endorsed the gifts, there appears to have been a decline in their usage and their occurrence. Almost every major personality of church history had some exposure to and acceptance of signs and wonders."[18]

Didache (90-120)

The Didache (The Teaching) was a Greek handbook of instructions concerning church order and morals. It does not speak specifically of signs and wonders, but speaks at length about apostles and prophets and their conduct in the local churches.

Justin Martyr (100 -165)

Justin was a Christian apostle of the beginning of the second century.

Quote, "For numberless demoniacs throughout the whole world, and in your city, many of our Christian men exercising them in the name of Jesus Christ.. And do heal rendering helpless and driving out the possessing devils out of the men." [19]

A further quote from Justin is the following, "for the prophetical gifts remain with us, even to the present time.."[20]

---

[18] Wimber, John; Notes from "Signs & Wonders and Church Growth; 6:1
[19] Coxe, A. Cleveland. The Ante-Nicene Fathers; Eerdmans, Grand Rapids. 1951 (6:190)
[20] IBID 1:240

Irenaeus (140-203)
Bishop of Lyons.

Quote, "For some do certainly and truly drive out devils, so that those who have been cleansed from evil spirits frequently join themselves to the church. Others have foreknowledge of things to come: they see visions, and utter prophetic expressions. Others still, heal the sick by laying their hands upon them, and they are made whole. Yea, moreover, as I have said, the dead even have been raised up, and remained among us for many years. And what shall I more say..."[21]

Tertullian (160-220)
a third century apostle and prolific writer.

"How many men.. have been delivered from devils, and healed of diseases. Even Severus himself, the father of Antonine... was mindful of the Christians that are in gratitude for his having once cured him by anointing. [22]

Hippolytus (d. 236)
A presbyter and teacher in the church at Rome. Wrote The Apostolic Tradition; In the section "Of a Gift of Healing" he says,

"If anyone among the laity appear to have received a gift of healing by revelation, hands shall not be laid on him because the matter is manifest."

Concerning the demonized, Hippolytus suggests, "..but if there be one who has a devil, let him not hear the word teacher until he has been cleansed." [23]

---

[21] IBID 1:409
[22] IBID 3:107
[23] Dix, Gregory; The Treatise of the Apostolic Tradition. SPCK London; P. 24

Antony (251-356)

Our knowledge of Anthony depends largely on his biography, written by Athanasius shortly after his death. Antony says, "We must not boast of casting out devils, not be elated at the healing of diseases, nor should we admire only the men who casts out devils, and account that one useless who does not." His biography is still available today and makes a very interesting read, especially chapters 39 through 42. [24]

Augustine (354- 430)

Cessationists quote Augustine's earlier work which sounds like he is a convinced cessationist, but in his later writings he gives detailed testimony of many miracles that he personally witnessed, as well as having prayed for some of them himself.

I will quote one example, "The miracle which was wrought at Milan when I was there, and by which a blind man was restored to sight, could come to the knowledge of many; for not only is the city a large one, but also the emperor was there at the time, and the occurrence was witnessed by an immense concourse of people.." [25]

Gregory of Tours (538-594)

Bishop of Tours and a prolific writer; wrote seven books on miracles with many accounts of healings which were occurring in his time and detailed accounts of casting out demons. [26]

---

[24] Defferari, Joseph; The Fathers of The Church; Vol. 15:169-174
[25] Augustine; City of God 22:8; available at
<http://www.newadvent.org/fathers/120122.htm>

Bede (673-735)

Bede was an English monk and prolific writer. In his book, <u>Bede, His Life, Times and Writings</u>, chapter seven is entitled <u>Bede's Miracle Stories</u>, is filled with miracles and healings.

To save time, I will mention a few only by name even though they are important figures and their books easily obtained. Bernard of Clairvaux (1090-1153) Francis of Assisi (1181-1226) Vincent Ferrer (1350-1419) Ignatius of Loyola (1491-1556) Theresa of Avila and John of The Cross (16 c.)

Groups, split off from the Roman Catholic Church, who experienced and wrote about the supernatural power of God, were the Albigensians of Southern France; Bogomiles of Bulgaria.

The Waldensian movement spread during the middle ages, had specific doctrinal instructions for the healing of the sick through the anointing with oil. They believed in visions, prophesies and deliverance from demonic possession. These groups were seriously persecuted by the Roman Church in an attempt to exterminate them.

We see, therefore, that the argument for cessationism ignores both the Bible and history and is built totally on personal lack of experience. "I have seen no miracles therefore, there are none." Several denominations have actually rewritten their own history, deleting all record of the healings and deliverances accomplished by their founders and early followers pretending that these things

---

[26] Defferan, 39:170-173

never occurred. I believe the foregoing offers sufficient proof that supernatural healing, deliverances and miracles never ceased and were experienced in all of Church history.

BIBLIOGRAPHY

Bosworth, Fred;   *Christ The Healer*
Blue, Ken;   *Authority To Heal*
Hagin, Kenneth, E. *Seven Things You Should Know About Divine Healing*
Kenyon, E.W.   *Jesus The Healer*
Lindsay, Gordon;   *Why Christians Are Sick*
Lindsay, Gordon;   *John G. Lake, Sermons on Dominion over Demons, Disease and Death*
McCrossan, T. J.   *Bodily Healing and the Atonement*
Murray, Andrew;   *Divine Healing*
Murray, Andrew;   *The Power of The Blood*
Wimber, John;   *Signs and Wonder and Church Growth*
Whyte, Maxwell;   *Dominion Over Demons*
Yeomans, Lillian;   *Health and Healing*
Wright, N.T.   *Simply Christian*

AFTERWORD

It is my sincere prayer that the Holy Spirit will illuminate your mind to embrace these wonderful life changing truths from God's word.

Since these teachings are controversial in some circles I am willing to dialogue concerning anything in these pages. However, I must insist that any argument be based on chapter and verse of God's word and not be based on your experience. Any communications offered in a spirit of meekness, love and scriptural integrity will be replied to. Or if you desire prayer for healing, email me at: **elaustro008@gmail.com**

I echo the apostle Paul's prayer for you—

EPH 1:16 [I] *do not cease to give thanks for you, making mention of you in my prayers: 17 that the God of our Lord Jesus Christ, the Father of glory, may give to you the spirit of wisdom and revelation in the knowledge of Him, 18 the eyes of your understanding being enlightened; that you may know what is the hope of His calling, what are the riches of the glory of His inheritance in the saints, 19 and what is the exceeding greatness of His power toward us who believe, according to the working of His mighty power 20 which He worked in Christ when He raised Him from the dead and seated Him at His right hand in the heavenly places,*
21 far above all principality and power and might and dominion, and every name that is named, not only in this age but also in that which is to come. 22 And He put all things under His feet, and gave Him to be head over all things to the church, 23 which is His body, the fullness of Him who fills all in all.

In Him

Pablo

Made in the USA
Monee, IL
16 February 2021

60669705R00094